"I never thought that I'd see it—an upbeat, all-you-ever-wanted-to-know guide to working in temporary jobs. Deborahann Smith's enthusiasm is infectious, and she has tips galore for temps, showing that far from being a trap, it can be a very positive experience."

—MILTON MOSKOWITZ, author of *The 100 Best Companies to Work For in America*

"Smith, a freelance writer and long-time temporary employee, provides facts and opinions about temping in a witty and amiable fashion. Her information and insights do much to dispel the notion that temping is a second-rate form of employment and means of career development. . . . This is a little book packed with big ideas. It's one of the first resources available on the topic and belongs in every library's career section."

—ALAN FARBER, *Library Journal*

TEMP

HOW TO SURVIVE AND THRIVE IN THE WORLD OF TEMPORARY EMPLOYMENT

Deborahann Smith

Shambhala
Boston & London
1994

C. 1

Shambhala Publications, Inc.
Horticultural Hall
300 Massachusetts Avenue
Boston, Massachusetts 02115

© 1994 by Deborahann Smith

9 8 7 6 5 4 3 2 1
First Edition

Printed in the United States of America on acid-free paper ♾

Distributed in the United States by Random House, Inc.,
and in Canada by Random House of Canada Ltd

Library of Congress Cataloging-in-Publication Data
Smith, Deborahann, 1955–
    Temp: how to survive and thrive in the world of temporary
employment / Deborahann Smith. — 1st ed.
      p.   cm.
    ISBN 0-87773-934-X (acid-free paper)
    1. Temporary employment.   I. Title.
HD5854.S57   1994   93-28072
650.14—dc20   CIP

To all the companies and people who have gifted me with the experiences of this book first-hand. And to past, present and future temporary workers everywhere.

CONTENTS

ACKNOWLEDGMENTS

I mention in *Temp* that an important aspect of temporary work is to "be excellent" to people encountered along the way. In the same vein, I would like to be excellent to those who contributed to the existence of this book: to Ann Morehead for suggesting temporary work (and for sending flowers through the mail); to Jerry Cleveland for endlessly listening, and urging me to transfer the experiences to paper; to Vala Hudspeth, fellow temp, for sharing both laughter and tears; to Merl Brotzman for befriending me on my fourth assignment; to Hobart Bell of the Boulder Zen Center for encouraging me to be a cheerful hellion; to Jonathan Green of Shambhala Publications for his enthusiasm about the manuscript; to Kendra Crossen of Shambhala Publications for patiently sculpting my words into a real book; and to all of the Shambhala staff for their expertise and support.

I would also like to show excellence to my parents, without whom this book would be impossible, of course; to Gladys A. Frumpworth IV for consenting to be my alter ego; and to all my friends everywhere—their names are herein printed in indelible (not temporary) invisible ink.

TEMP

❖ ❖ ❖

INTRODUCTION

W hen I was five my friends and I sat in the mulberry tree in my backyard, watching a bright blue dragonfly and fantasizing about what we would be when we grew up. Scott was going to be a teacher like his father. Susie wanted to be a veterinarian. Joanne vacillated between ballerina and movie star, and Michael dreamed of racing motorcycles. At the time, I couldn't conceive of being an adult, let alone having a career. Even first grade seemed a million years away. I was more interested in the dragonfly as it gracefully landed on a branch, looked around, fluttered its iridescent wings ever so slightly, ascended to the next branch, and finally flew away. No, I didn't really know what to be when I grew up, but I remember thinking at that moment that it would be wonderful to be a dragonfly.

At the age of seven I decided to be a writer. I had been in school for two years by then, and understood this to be a more realistic career. I scared my teachers with stories of green witches, spotted goblins, and house-sized spiders. They said my imagination gave them the creeps, and sent me outside to play.

After college I watched my friends and myself become what we wanted to be when we grew up. I wrote feature articles for university magazines and published short stories on the side. My long-time friend Kathy was named production manager of a major newspaper. Peter returned to school to pursue a Ph.D. in psychology. We all vowed to excel in our careers. We would have fancy offices and important titles, make lots of money, and buy lots of "stuff." In our magnificent scheming, our paths were straightforward, with no hidden forks. It didn't occur to us that perhaps we would attain our goals via an alternate route, or that we might discover new opportunities altogether. Certainly we never considered that one of us would grow up to be something we hadn't thought of—a "temp."

Like many people who do temporary work, I kind of fell into it. Previously, I'd had ten years of so-called permanent jobs, mostly in publishing. I'd also taught preschool, done counseling in a county jail, and survived two months on an assembly line, where I developed a severe personality conflict with a drill press. When I decided to take the plunge into freelance writing six years ago, my plan was to write full-time. I had contracted to write travel guidebooks and a few catalogues and brochures. This worked for a year. When I discovered that I needed additional income to fill in the gaps, it appeared that I might have to return to the permanent workaday world.

The option of temping never crossed my mind until my friend Ann suggested it as a solution to my problem. I could find work quickly, she pointed out. I could write when I wanted to and work when I needed to. I could travel and find temporary assignments in any city I visited. The more Ann talked, the more appealing the idea of doing temporary work became. Thus my new career began.

I soon discovered that I wasn't alone. As I wove in and out of businesses, I met dozens of other temporary workers who were traveling from job to job. At first it seemed incredible that so many temping opportunities actually existed, but I soon realized that there were a number of reasons why employers seek out temporary help:

❖ A regular employee is on vacation, maternity leave, or disability leave for a short period of time.
❖ The validity of a certain position is being tested.
❖ A position is geared specifically toward one project, which may be covered by a grant or government contract.
❖ Employers are cutting back on expensive benefits such as health insurance, holidays, paid sick leave, vacations, and pensions, which they don't generally pay to temporary workers.
❖ Employers want to assess an employee as a temp before making a commitment.
❖ Employers can't financially commit to a long-term position, so they "make do" on a temporary basis.

While this may sound like bad news for employees, it is actually good news for people who play the temporary job field. Temps can take advantage of the flexibility and variety that temporary employment offers, while job hunting or taking a breather from career burn-out. Short-term assignments provide an opportunity to remain financially fit between long-term projects or while making decisions about a new career direction. Temps who enjoy travel can work through a temporary service in almost any city they visit. Temporary positions offer exposure to different companies and fields. Every kind of business at some point uses temporary help.

As a new member of this pool of temps, I was drawn to any information I could find on the subject. A December 1991 article in the *Wall Street Journal* stated that 25 percent of all new positions are being assigned on a temporary, contract, or consulting basis. In March 1993, *Time* magazine reported that 1.5 million temps are dispatched daily from temporary agencies, and an additional 34 million people work on some sort of contingency basis. The same article pointed out that contingent workers (freelancers, independent contractors, part-timers, and temps) occupied one quarter of the work force in 1988, and this figure is expected to *double* by the year 2000! Not surprisingly, I also learned that between 1975 and 1987, the number of temporary help agencies in the United States increased by 239 percent. Manpower Temporary Services alone assigned over one million workers worldwide in 1990, and the temporary services market in the United States for that same year grossed $15 billion in sales.

Armed with these facts, I saw myself in a new and positive light. I was not merely a drifter wandering through a series of odd jobs, I was one of a number of professional people who were consciously taking advantage of temporary work as a rewarding way of life.

My transition into temping required some personal adjustments. I had to learn to be more flexible and versatile. I had to learn to be less self-centered, and more concerned with the welfare of others. I had to realize the importance of mindfully applying myself to every job, no matter how minor a task seemed to be. On a practical level, I also needed to review how much money I needed to survive. But most of all, temping demanded that I go *beyond* what my past experiences had taught me—including the security of staying with one company, with supportive co-workers, and writing within the safety of my home. I had been used to knowing my way around my own small world. The more I ventured out, the more I felt a sense of the world as a larger place—an interconnection of companies and groups of people. Because I was at each company for such a short duration, I became more aware of the passage of time, more aware of the presence of each moment. It also occurred to me that in "flying" from business to business I had become the dragonfly after all!

Gradually, I began to view myself as part of a larger scheme. I thought of all the other temps who were making similar adjustments in their lives, and wondered: as a society, was it possible to accept temporary employment as a continuing trend? Could there be more general education to help businesses and individuals harmoniously interweave permanent and temporary positions in the workplace? Could some information be developed to give temporary workers moral support?

As I did temporary work, I searched for guidance. I wanted specifics about short-term versus long-term assignments, negotiating hours and wages, and the best ways to communicate with agencies and businesses. I wanted advice to steer me through transitions, holidays, job lulls, and jealous co-workers. I was curious to know if there was a temp "protocol" in this business of traveling through jobs. Unfortunately, my search yielded very few answers. As I temped, it never occurred to me that I was gathering my own information, providing my own guidance. I just temped, learning by trial and error—and by the seat of my paisley pants.

One hundred companies later, I realized that I had a bowlful of adventures to make a book out of—a recipe for temping that somehow worked. This is it. My wish is for others to discover the same advantages that have turned my experiences into a new taste for life.

GETTING STARTED

WHAT IS A TEMP?

I'm glad you asked. By definition, a temp is

❖ Someone who enters a work situation for a specific period of time—a week, a month, or whatever the arrangement is
❖ Someone who maintains the workload until a permanent employee returns
❖ Someone who steps in until a suitable replacement can be found for a particular position
❖ Someone who lends an extra hand to a project
❖ Someone who moves on to help another company when the assignment is completed

In addition, a temp may be hired for a special project, or on a seasonal basis. For instance, my friend Ian once folded five hundred flyers into airplanes for an airline's promotional package, and another friend, Valerie, has worked many summers at a gardening center. Yes, a temp plays many different roles.

Other than the defined time factor involved in temporary work, there is little to distinguish a temp from a permanent employee. After all, everyone hopes to obtain the same basics from a work situation: an honest livelihood, job satisfaction, rapport with co-workers, respect from co-workers, feelings of productivity and usefulness, and opportunities for personal and professional growth. The difference is that permanent workers receive these basics from a single job, while temps draw from many. But temping goes beyond adding an extra hand or "holding down the fort." It's also about helping people to feel positive about themselves and their work. Being a temp means being willing to be present in each assignment, no matter what it is, and give whatever is necessary to the job. It means being willing to go outside of yourself, to offer

7

complete attention to the task, whether it requires executing drawings for a water management program or dressing up as Snackie the Clown and distributing honey-coated peanuts at a shopping mall. Temping means being cheerful even if you were a manager in your last job, or the Queen of Egypt in your last life. Being a temp is actually a more involved job than most people think.

But can you really satisfy these needs by working at so many jobs? you might ask. *Can you be personally fulfilled when you're only on an assignment for a short period of time?* Sure. For me, job satisfaction and growth are stimulated by a variety of activities and people interaction, both of which are fulfilled by temping. In fact, I actually feel more creative because my imagination is inspired by new and different experiences. My most difficult adjustment has been learning to take responsibility for my own satisfaction, to be an active participant, to make it happen. By being willing to involve myself a little more quickly in the give and take of the situation, I earn respect, and create rapport with my co-workers.

Okay, you may agree, *but don't you get jobs that are outside of your field, that are tedious or "beneath" you?* It's true that sometimes I am assigned dull tasks. I've noticed that everyone complains at times about work, however, no matter what their job description is—myself included. I've had highly responsible, flexible, creative jobs. I've had boring, inflexible jobs. The truth is that I've been unhappy in both at one time or another. This makes me wonder if I can recognize the potential in each situation—even the tasks I initially feel are "beneath" me. I may also choose to view repetitive tasks such as photocopying as opportunities to keep me aware of where I am, to experience life in this very moment.

I can see your point, you might say, *but do you feel embarrassed to admit that you're a temp?* In the beginning this was confusing because I was used to having some kind of title that people could relate to, that indicated a specific role. I had been a writer, a creative director, a teacher. These labels said something, or so I thought. "Temp" wasn't a title that people readily understood. I mean, how could I go to a party and explain that this week I walked around as a carrot to advertise a new vegetarian restaurant? Or that last week I FedEx'ed extra shirts and underwear to someone whose business trip was unexpectedly extended? I thought that people wouldn't take me seriously if I talked about some of my temporary assignments. Now I don't worry about it. I just admit that I am a temp. My work involves moving from job to job. So far this has included

Cashiering at university bookstores
Puppeteering at a toy store
Arranging flowers
Substitute-teaching
Processing photographs in a darkroom
Writing résumés
Editing catalogues
Indexing technical manuals
Cleaning houses
Executing technical drawings
Answering telephones

and performing no end of computer work in various and sundry companies across the United States. The last time I counted, these added up to over one hundred businesses, ranging in tenure from a half day to four months. I can truthfully say that, as a temp, I've learned something about people or work from each of these jobs, and I expect to learn more.

You might nod your head now and say that you never thought of it quite that way, but still, you point out, *there is the very real question of paid benefits.* Yes, the lack of paid benefits for temps—notably vacations, health insurance, and retirement plans—is a legitimate concern. Temporary agencies provide options for some of these benefits, and other alternatives do exist. This is such an important subject that it has its own chapter in this book. But please remember that there can be emotional benefits to temping, such as flexibility, variety, and the chance to seriously help someone out. A major turning point for me in this area was a two-month assignment for a woman who'd had a mastectomy. She was so grateful to me for covering her desk that I felt like my being there wasn't just a job, but a significant contribution.

Speaking of emotions, you may return, *aren't you unnerved by the constant change that temporary work entails?* You're right, temping takes a little getting used to. It requires a different way of viewing employment. To most of us, the idea of change is frightening. Instead of allowing it to be an avenue for growth, we see it as an obstacle on our familiar path—especially when applied to something as vital as work. But if we stop to examine even our "permanent" jobs, we realize that many changes and unknowns exist there as well. New policies are established. New products are developed. People come and go. We move from one position to another, from one job to another. By taking this perspective, we realize that we constantly succeed at the change that we are so afraid of!

At its best, being a temp reminds me of my favorite kind of story, the "characters in an elevator" story, in which two or more very different kinds of people enter an elevator, the doors close, and the elevator has a long ride or—even better—gets stuck between floors. The characters must then somehow relate to each other inside that small square of space, inside that small square of time. They have no choice but to communicate and work toward a common goal. When the elevator doors finally open, the occupants are changed, even if only a little. They have gained a new perspective and understanding, or have learned something important about how other people live that they can carry along on their life journey.

At one temporary job of mine, I actually became one of the "characters in an elevator." I was in a skyscraper in New York, traveling from the lobby to the top floor. When I entered the elevator, a tall Jamaican man in a tweed hat also stepped aboard. He carried a dark blue plate with a steaming artichoke in the center. Next to the artichoke was a small white cup of hot melted butter. On that ride, the man taught me how to tear off an artichoke leaf, dip it into butter, and scrape the pulp off with my teeth, using my tongue as a guide—an exotic experience, to say the least. When we reached my floor, I thanked him and got off. He responded with a wide, white grin and tipped his hat. And although I often looked for him after that, I never saw the artichoke man again.

This is what being a temp is about. You enter an unknown space and come out with a taste of something new. It is an opportunity to meet a variety of characters, to have experiences different from what you might normally encounter during the course of your daily life. In the elevator and out—and off to another assignment.

WHO TEMPS?

After temping for a few weeks at a company that develops software for NASA, I suddenly noticed an older man who dressed mainly in gray. He never spoke or made eye contact with anyone, just moved quietly through the halls, always carrying a trash can to the bin outside. One day an engineer came to my desk and asked if I'd seen "Joe." I knew I hadn't met a "Joe," but thought for a minute and remembered that I had recently seen the trash can man heading up the stairs.

"Joe?" I asked. "You mean the janitor?"

The engineer immediately exploded into laughter. It turned out that Joe wasn't the janitor at all. He was (a) a software designer, and—gulp—(b) *a temp.*

The adage "You can't judge a book by its cover" may never have had a more apt application than to temporary workers. Disguised under the simple cover of the label "temp" is a vast variety of people. Indeed, temporary workers come from many different career fields, educational backgrounds, and lifestyles. They are men and women. They are married and single. They are parents and grandparents. Some have Ph.D.'s. Some have G.E.D.'s. They are recent graduates or experienced business owners looking for new careers. They are between jobs or school semesters, or are looking for extra cash after they retire. Temps are new mothers, using short-term assignments as stepping stones back into the full-time workaday world.

Some temps are travelers, working on the road. My friend Sue is such a traveler. She has an advanced degree in psychology but is temporarily cleaning houses with the goal of saving enough money to go to South America. As she cleans, she listens to Spanish language tapes. Her clients don't ask about her background. As far as they are concerned, she is just "the housecleaner." Sue doesn't mind. If someone asks what she does for a living, she says, "I am a traveler, wandering through life." She assumes that she will play many more roles as the years go by.

There are temps who view short-term situations as cushions to support their art or particular passion in life. For instance, there are folks who work during the summer and ski during the winter, and folks who kayak all summer, then work all winter. Still other people see temping as an opportunity to broaden their horizons, to be exposed to a variety of businesses and people. All are attracted to the flexibility that temporary work affords. They are circulating in the work force by the millions.

Here are the profiles of some other temps that I have met along the way.

Sharon, in her late forties, with grown children, is between jobs and looking for a high-level administrative position. Temping gives her insight and exposure to future employers.

Hilary, in her late twenties, and the daughter of a well-known novelist, temps to make ends meet while she sets up a marketing business in her home.

Clark was a law library research assistant for seven years before burning out and turning to temporary work. Married, with an infant, he is on the lookout for a new career.

Ed was laid off by his company after twenty years. He decided to use the opportunity to pursue his lifelong interest in law enforcement. He works temporary while taking classes to help fulfill his dream.

Valerie says that she's "worked as an accountant for practically more years than I've been alive." She now alternates temping with traveling and Zen retreats.

Tina is fluent in four languages. She works temporary word-processing and telemarketing jobs in conjunction with doing translation work and teaching.

Art, in his late forties, with two teenagers, is an engineer who is working on his doctorate in computer science. After leaving his last job because of irreconcilable differences with a superior, he takes a temporary position with a communications company. He is eventually hired as a permanent employee.

Jim is a retired air traffic controller. He does part-time temporary work to keep active and to make a little cash. He also takes off several months a year to ski or play golf.

Lucy, single, in her late thirties, has moved to a new city and is seeking a position in publication graphics. She finds herself playing temporary roles that she never dreamed of, such as architect's assistant, clown, and window dresser.

Carol is a sixty-year-old grandmother who has moved around the United States for more than twenty-five years. During this time she has worked for one temporary agency, which transferred her records from city to city. As a temp, she has been a legal secretary, demonstrated toys, served food samples, and "answered half the world's telephones."

As you can see, temps come from many walks of life. They are in transition, "walking" from one situation to another. And speaking of walks, I am reminded of an eight-year-old boy and a small white dog that I met recently on the street.

"Cute dog," I commented as we waited on a corner for the light to change.

"Thanks," he replied. "But it's not my dog. I have a company. I walk dogs for a quarter. Of course, I won't be doing it in the fall because I'll be back in school and I won't have time. I'll be in third grade, and I heard that there will be homework this year."

So there you have it. A temporary worker may even come in the form of an eight-year-old entrepreneur!

ARE YOU TEMP MATERIAL?

I sometimes joke that I became tough after I started doing temporary work; it's true that frequent transitions tend to thicken your skin. To reinforce this idea, I created an alter ego: Gladys A. Frumpworth IV, "the Temp from Hell."

Gladys appeared in my life a few months into my temping career. She isn't called the Temp from Hell because she is hellacious, but because she knows her own mind and lives by it, a quality that people often fear. If she disagrees with the motivation of a business (e.g., nuclear power plants), she won't take the job. If she feels uncomfortable with certain skills (such as operating telephone switchboards), she won't accept an assignment. She believes that everyone deserves respect, no matter what.

Gladys is the type of person who had screaming red hair and a gravelly voice from the day of birth. She has bright green eyes and a mischievous grin. She is a no-nonsense worker who applies herself to everything with gusto. At the same time, Gladys is basically kind. She has always, her whole life, felt a great responsibility to justice for all. When she was twelve, she organized a group of junior high students to picket a local dime store because she felt that the pets were being mistreated. The protest was televised and the store was forced to clean up its act.

As the Temp from Hell, Gladys A. Frumpworth IV is truly temp material. She knows that the key to temping is attitude, plain and simple. It's cheerfully pitching in and doing the work. It's paying attention to the quality of the task. To Gladys, temping is also about learning to play the game. She first approaches an assignment with caution. She listens, observes, learns. After a while, she figures out the written rules, the unwritten rules, and the places where she can bend the rules. She learns where she fits in and where she doesn't. Sometimes she's a savior, but she's not always the piece that nicely completes the company jigsaw puzzle. That's okay, because she's flexible, but also self-defined.

Of course, it isn't necessary to be exactly like Gladys to succeed at temporary work, but a few of her qualities are worth emulating. A positive attitude and flexibility are imperative. A good sense of humor and the willingness to stand up for yourself will make assignments easier. But don't worry if you don't have all of these qualities, Gladys says. Chances are that you will acquire them along the way.

Would you describe yourself as:

❖ Having a positive outlook on life?
❖ Flexible?
❖ Assertive?
❖ Independent?
❖ A go-getter?
❖ People-oriented?
❖ Self-disciplined?
❖ Having a strong self-image?
❖ Having a good sense of humor, including the ability to laugh at yourself?
❖ Having the ability to learn new things quickly?
❖ Able to live on a shoestring, if necessary?
❖ In good physical health?
❖ Willing to set emotional boundaries for yourself and others?
❖ Willing to take instructions and to ask questions?
❖ Adventurous about new situations and people?

If you answered yes to most of these questions, you are a likely candidate for temporary work. It means that you have the ability to insert yourself into a new environment and navigate within it because you enjoy meeting new people and can quickly assess a situation. It means that you are willing to figure out what needs to be done and do it, whether working on your own or taking instructions from others or learning something new. It also means that you have enough self-respect to be assertive about getting new assignments, and to not let people take advantage of you. On a practical level, you are realistic about financial and health constraints—your cash flow can survive job lulls and you don't take assignments that jeopardize your health.

On the other hand, you may want to postpone the temporary employment option if you answer yes to any of these questions:

❖ Are you strongly territorial?
❖ Do you have a tendency to take things very personally?
❖ Are you extremely shy?
❖ Do you feel great distress over being asked to switch gears in the middle of a project?
❖ Do you have a lot of financial overhead—car and house payments, credit card debts, or ongoing medical expenses?
❖ Do you have dependents at home?
❖ Have you recently undergone a major change or personal crisis in your life, such as a divorce, serious illness, or death in your family?

These issues are important to address before embarking on a temporary career. I've known temps who would have been happier in permanent jobs until their personal circumstances stabilized a bit. People with many ongoing expenses, dependents, or chronic illnesses are under enough pressure without adding the transitions of temporary work to their concerns. And those who are undergoing personal crises might be more comfortable in a consistently supportive environment. Times of stress are simply not conducive to the kind of emotional weight-training that temporary work provides.

Personally, I have enjoyed temping over the past few years, but there have been periods in my life when I needed more stability, when I felt territorial and shy, when I had larger financial burdens. I have no doubt that the temp experience would have been more detrimental than positive during those times.

Gladys A. Frumpworth IV has truly saved me on many days. If I'm feeling vulnerable on an assignment, I invoke Gladys. I remind myself of her gravelly pay-attention voice and the no-nonsense way that she carries herself as she claims the halls. I remember the protest at the pet store, the basic attitude that everyone deserves kindness and justice. In my mind, she takes whatever form is necessary to get her message across. Sometimes she looms ten feet over my head. Sometimes she is small enough to fit inside my pocket. Other times she transports herself on little wings and whispers words of wisdom into my ear to get me through difficult days. Or she laughs merrily and reminds me to lighten up.

If you choose to do temporary work, it helps to have the attitude that working temporary is okay, that you are open to whatever comes along. The truth is that you have to be a bit of a daredevil to temp. You have to be willing to take some emotional and financial risks, even if you plan to temp for a short tenure. Transitions can be fatiguing, and job lulls are possible. Long-term temps are motivated by something more than a regular schedule and "real money." The flexibility of the temporary lifestyle or living out a personal passion (such as a writing career) is more important to them than paid vacations and holidays and retirement plans. It is even more important than paid health insurance. These temps are willing to step off the beaten path and face the unknown—again and again and again.

So, to temp or not to temp? Is this the question for you? It's worth a frank discussion with yourself. And if you're not certain, but are still tempted to take the plunge, perhaps Gladys can guide you along the way.

HOW AND WHERE TO BEGIN

Have you ever thought of your job as a smorgasbord? No, I didn't think you had. But this is what temporary employment is about. Imagine a long table, covered with all kinds of dishes. You travel its length, choosing the foods that appeal to you, leaving the rest for others. If you're like Gladys, you'll grab the baked brie and marinated chili peppers, and pass by the cold cuts and olives. *You* pick and choose. Sometimes your favorites are already taken, and you have to settle for your second favorites until the plates are refilled. Sometimes the condiments aren't spicy enough. There may be more junk food than you're used to. Even so, if you look at the entire table, there are many choices. Where do you begin?

Once you make the decision to do temporary work, you have to find a place to start. So, now that I've made you hungry, fix yourself an avocado and cheddar sandwich, and consider the following questions.

What are your reasons for doing temporary work? New in town . . . need a job *quick* . . . picking up extra money between jobs . . . exploring businesses before deciding on a long-term situation . . . traveling . . . supplementing your basic income . . . supporting your art form . . . ? If you're clear about your reasons, you're more likely to find the right situation.

What kind of temporary work do you expect to do? Office administration . . . accounting . . . legal assistance . . . word processing . . . computer programming . . . day labor . . . babysitting . . . housecleaning . . . construction . . . health care . . . food service . . . ? There are many possibilities. Seasonal work is plentiful—retail during the holidays, or agricultural work, forest service jobs, landscaping, lifeguarding, road-flagging and camp-counseling during the summer.

Can you take advantage of personal experiences and skills? Make a list of your previous experiences, including volunteer positions, classes, and hobbies. Most people are amazed at how many skills they have when they think about it. Forgotten skills may qualify you for more employment openings than you think. For example, Gladys netted her first floral designing projects on the basis of her personal interest in flower arranging.

Have you researched all the options? Be resourceful. Read articles about the areas you're planning to pursue. Talk to people who have worked in this capacity. Talk to agencies. Check the library for information about a particular field or occupation. Pay attention to job fairs that are held in your area.

What is the best way to approach this work? Temporary employment agency . . . ads in the paper . . . index cards or flyers on bulletin boards in a university, food co-op, or other community center . . . cold-calling . . . personal contacts . . .

You might talk to people that you've met through jobs, or respond to an advertisement in the paper, or place your own ad. I know one temp who read the classified listings for administrative jobs, then called the businesses and offered herself as a stand-in until a full-time employee could be hired. Another temp went door to door at a large office building, promoting herself as a stand-in receptionist for vacations. Armed with her résumé, substantial references, and a great deal of charm, she managed to keep herself in business for an entire summer and fall.

I use my personal contacts whenever possible, especially when I travel to cities where I have friends. Usually somebody has a lead about somebody else who can use some help for a week or two. In this way, I give the business a hand and pay for my trip at the same time. The key rule here is to remember that you are offered the jobs based on your friends' reputations. Therefore, treat such assignments the same way that you would treat the friends who gave you the job lead—with great respect.

How much money do you require to survive? Of course it's prudent to match financial requirements to the work you plan to do. Since there are sometimes gaps between assignments, it can be a balancing act to make certain that cash flow is adequate. I think it's safe to assume that worrying about finances is nobody's favorite pastime.

Can you be easily contacted? This is crucial, since most temporary work is available on a "first come, first served" basis. Will you be home to answer the phone? Do you have an answering machine? If you're new in town and don't have your own telephone, can you be reached through a friend or answering service?

How will you get to assignments? Do you have a car? Are the job sites accessible via foot or public transportation? Are cabs available if the business is located in a remote area and you have to work late at night? If the job is in a city that you are unfamiliar with, do you have a map? It also helps to have the closest subway stop or bus route number.

Do you have a Social Security card, birth certificate, driver's license, or proof of naturalized citizenship? The law requires proof of American citizenship or a work visa (if you are from another country) to work in the United States.

Are you willing to commute or relocate? Sometimes temporary work is more available in urban areas or other geographical locales. Salaries also tend to be higher in cities and in certain areas of the country.

Do you have computer skills? Much of today's temporary employment involves the use of computers, and that's where some of the highest pay lies. If you don't have experience, you can gain it by getting a friend to teach you some basics . . . taking classes through a vocational-technical institute or adult education . . . practicing on tutorial programs through your temporary agency . . . using quick-reference "cheat" books, such as *WordPerfect Quick Reference* by Que or *Microsoft Word for the IBM PC* by Microsoft Press . . . studying one program and applying what you've learned to similar programs.

Are you willing to do phones? Telephone work is the place where many people begin their careers as temps. There is a high turnover in receptionist jobs, so they are available in abundance. They also act as good foot-in-the-door assignments for temps who are looking for permanent work. When Gladys first began temping, a receptionist at a Fortune 500 company shared the following tips:

❖ Write out the name of the company and information about it, and keep it by the phone so that you remember which business you're at.
❖ Be courteous.
❖ Don't be afraid to ask people to repeat their names or numbers.
❖ Don't eat, chew gum, or deep-breathe into the phone (which that rascal Gladys was tempted to do, but she resisted!).

Do you plan to temp long-term? If you are considering a long-term situation and will be working through a temporary agency, it may be in your best interest to remain with one agency, since benefits are often available in exchange for working over a longer period of time. Research agencies to discover which one will best satisfy your needs.

Are you willing to market yourself? Sometimes the best jobs come through sheer assertiveness. Keep your eyes open. Answer ads, call your friends and ex-employers, and contact your temporary agency. Read the next chapter. Be available.

In short, there are many tasty items on the temporary-work smorgasbord table, and if you're the first in line, finding the baked brie and marinated chili peppers usually isn't a problem—that is, if Gladys left some behind! Like anything else, temping is a matter of deciding which end of the table to start at, and keeping your eyes open for exactly what you want. It's deciding which appetizers you'll choose to satisfy your palate until the right entrée comes along. And it's also about risking some items on the table that you've never before tasted, items that you may actually discover are to your liking. The table is large and opportunities *do* exist, assures Gladys. Especially when you're hungry.

MARKET YOURSELF

F uturists predict that a large percentage of jobs that will exist ten years from now aren't even known to us today because the employment market is changing so rapidly. Personally, I like to think this means that we'll be temping on Mars in the next century, although it's possible to temp and still keep our feet on earth. In any case, whether on Mars or Earth, you can stay on top of the market by keeping up with trends and viewing yourself as a necessary "service" or "product." Then orbit yourself into a marketable position by taking these simple measures to fill current needs:

BE SELF-AWARE. Recognize who you are and where your skills lie. You are probably more talented than you think. Realize that you are a significant contributor to the work force. Keep in mind why you are doing temporary work and what your goals are. If you are "the Temp from Hell," remember this, and stick to your priorities.

TAKE INITIATIVES TO IMPROVE YOUR SKILLS. Visualize your ultimate goal, and seize every opportunity to achieve it, whether in the form of classes, seminars, experimenting with software on an assignment, or doing volunteer work. Be on the lookout for anything that might aid you in your goal. Talk to people while on assignments. Someone may have skills, knowledge, or experiences that can be of benefit to you.

ACQUIRE UNIVERSAL SKILLS. Good verbal and written communication, listening skills, problem-solving, and computer proficiency are a few qualifications that every business is looking for.

KEEP UP WITH JOB MARKET TRENDS. Read current newspapers, business publications, and trade magazines to gain new ideas about new areas to branch into.

HAVE A POSITIVE ATTITUDE. This statement could become a broken record, but let's face it, people would rather work with someone who is pleasant than with a grouch. Yes, they would rather work with a cheerful hellion like Gladys A. Frumpworth IV. Also, if you're open-minded and willing to learn, employers are more likely to give you a chance at easing into new territories.

NETWORK. Be on the lookout for new contacts. Talk to people on the job. Talk to people at parties. You never know when someone will have interesting work. Gladys once found freelance work through a stranger sitting next to her on an airplane from Dallas to Cleveland. Keep in touch with old contacts. If you keep your name fresh in people's minds, you may be called when a project comes up.

BE ASSERTIVE AND PERSISTENT. Don't wait for employers to call you. Get on the telephone, knock on doors, write letters. Follow these up with second calls. Gladys once netted a job that had ninety other applicants because she was the only one who called back after the interview.

BE A SPECIALIST IN ONE OR TWO AREAS, BUT BE WILLING TO BRANCH OUT. Versatility is the name of the game in temporary work. Temps who count on one specialty may face more job lulls. The more areas you can branch into, the more assignments become available. This rule especially applies to computer-related positions.

CONNECT WITH LARGE COMPANIES. While small businesses offer a personal atmosphere, large companies have more opportunities available to temporary workers in the way of job openings (both temporary and permanent), classes and special activities, and advancement. Gladys temped at one corporation for five months, changing departments to replace workers on vacation, maternity leave, and so on. This offered her both the comfort of familiarity and the challenge of changing responsibilities—plus she got a chance to meet many other temps, who naturally formed a community of camaraderie and moral support.

Another important part of marketing yourself means just that: marketing your *self*. Selling your *self*. If you were selling spaceships, would you show tricycles to potential buyers? Temping is the same way. Before I met my alter ego, I role-played on temporary assignments. I thought this was what a temp did. In my mind, I was two people. In my nonwork time, I was me: a writer, walker, friend, lover, Zen student, social services volunteer, or whatever else I happened to be doing with my life at the moment. During the day, I was a "temp." I separated myself emotionally from the immediate environment. Consequently, my role connected with people at work, but *I* didn't.

"I'll play the role that the job calls for, then go home and be myself," I said out loud one day, as I faxed Singapore on my current assignment.

"Why not just be yourself all the time?" a little gravelly voice whispered in my ear. "Don't you think you will be happier, and other people will be more comfortable because they know who you are?"

"Who said that?" I demanded.

The little gravelly voice chuckled. It jumped off my shoulder, onto the floor, drew itself up to a full-sized woman, and initiated a hearty handshake. "Allow me to introduce myself," she said. After I stopped being blinded by her screaming red hair, I understood that this was Gladys A. Frumpworth IV, and that she would make sure I was myself on temporary jobs from then on. As usual, she was right.

So market your full self. Let people get to know you. Speak from the heart and soul of your experience. This doesn't mean talking about your unhappy childhood on the first day of an assignment. There is no need to divulge personal things at all if you don't want to. It simply means: allow your natural personality to shine through. Be genuine. Don't be just "the temp."

While self-marketing may sound like hard work, it is an important aspect of navigating through the competitive temporary job field. Admittedly, my marketing skills were weak in the beginning, but I've learned that it gets easier with experience. Also, Gladys assures me that being excellent on the job can be marketing in itself. I'll probably be a master at it, she says, by the time there is temping on Mars.

TEMPORARY AGENCIES

T here are temporary employment agencies for office administrators, accountants, travel agents, and assembly workers. There are agencies for engineers, electronics technicians, legal-system employees, graphic artists, health-care workers, and computer programmers. This only lists a few.

For fun, Gladys A. Frumpworth IV even started her own agency: Temps from Hell. On her card is a picture of a smiling devil brandishing a pitchfork. The devil has screaming red hair and bears a remarkable resemblance to Gladys, although she claims that it's entirely coincidence. "We're *Hot!*" the card proclaims. "We pitch in and do the work!" So far, Temps from Hell has two sure-fire employees. We have regular meetings for moral support. We have a devil of a good time.

Temporary agencies exist as go-betweens to match the skills of temporary workers to an employer's requirements. They are subject to government regulation concerning licensing, record-keeping, and reporting. In the United States, agencies are considered the legal employers of their temporary workers. They are governed by laws regulating the employer-employee relationship, including tax withholding or reporting, Social Security or retirement, antidiscrimination, and Workers' Compensation.

Agencies in the same field are competitive in wages. They make their money by charging the client 20–30 percent over what the temporary employee earns, although the temp never pays a fee. Temps can expect benefits ranging from paid holidays and vacation time, to stock-option plans and child care. (More specifics are listed in the "Benefits" chapter on page 30.)

Choosing which agency, and how many, to sign up with is arbitrary, unless you're in a specialty field. Many temps find success in playing "agency roulette"—applying at several, and seeing who calls first. Others favor one at a time. I've had positive results from using one agency as my main contact, with a second as backup. One advantage to this is that the people get to know you personally, which keeps your name more specifically in their minds. In addition, if you stay with one agency over a period of time, you may accrue enough hours to be eligible for extra incentives.

What's the procedure?

1. *Call for an appointment.* Except for Temps from Hell, temporary service offices are busy places, so it's best to have an appointment. Otherwise, you may have to wait awhile. Plan on an hour or so to fill out an application, interview, and review your résumé or portfolio. If applicable, you may be asked to take a few short tests (typing, computer expertise, math, spelling).

2. *Take two forms of identification and references.* You will be asked to fill out a W-4 form for tax purposes and to show two forms of identification (driver's license, Social Security card, birth certificate) as proof of U.S. citizenship. If you are a citizen of another country, you must show a work visa. Agencies also request that you provide names and telephone numbers of three past employers as references.

3. *Keep in touch with the agency.* Call daily to keep your name on the availability list.
4. *Keep apprised of the payment schedule.* The agency provides time cards, which are signed by both the temp and the client. Time cards can be mailed or hand-carried to the agency, usually on a weekly basis. Paychecks are also generally issued weekly.
5. *Take responsibility for yourself.* Agencies may provide work assignments, but it's equally important for temps to be responsible to themselves. Make certain that job sites and duties are satisfactory, and that paychecks are correct. Communicate with the agency when a job is ending, and when you're ready for a new assignment.

Agencies have their own personalities. Discover the one that works best for your personal needs. A service that is effective for one temp may not pan out for another, mostly because of individual skills and personality compatibility with the people in the agency. Different agencies attract different kinds of clients (e.g., high tech, publishing, government contractors, small versus large business). Because of this, switching services from time to time can keep temporary experiences fresh. I also know temps who have used the same agency for more than twenty years and feel no need to change.

On the other hand, some temps wish to cut out the go-between and work directly with a company. This can be beneficial to both parties—since the temp can make more money and the client can save money—but it's crucial to first check the rules. Contracts between agencies and client companies often limit such practices by requiring a grace period of three months to a year before a temp can work directly with the company. Ignoring these contracts can result in a legal tangle, or in burning a bridge with the agency.

What about bad experiences? Are temporary services sometimes difficult to deal with? Truthfully, Gladys and I have had few problems. In examining those problems, along with reports from other temps, we've concluded that such episodes are mostly due to a personality conflict or miscommunication with one individual at the local service office. Gladys recommends that if you have a miscommunication, first try to resolve it. If you find that you are having "irreconcilable differences," don't dwell on it, and sign up with another agency. Agencies, like temps, have their ups and downs. You might even return to the same agency a year later and find that it has radically changed.

Agencies are invaluable contacts. There is a true balancing act that they must perform to make client-temp relationships a success. A certain amount of teamwork is required. Like the Temps from Hell slogan, it involves pitching in and doing the work. You can find work from other sources, but agencies are always there when you need them again. Treat them well, and they will do the same for you.

MONEY

I overheard two temps talking on the bus one day.

"Hey! I haven't seen you for a while! You still over at Mega-bucks Corporation?"

"No, that job ended. Now I'm working for Nickelardia."

"Oh, yeah? Are you making real money?"

"Of course not. Are you?"

Laughter. "Are you kidding?"

Of course, "real money" is defined by each individual according to his or her basic needs. Realistically speaking, if these needs include a mansion, two Porsches, a trip to Paris every season, and lazy Friday night dinners at the Ritz, temporary work is probably not for you. While many temps are accustomed to a higher standard of living before they turn to temping, they discover that it is possible to earn a comfortable livelihood in the temp world, if they put their mind to it.

Salaries on temporary assignments depend on a number of factors:

❖ The type of work you are doing (with factory production and telephone reception in the low bracket, computer and technical skills at the high bracket)
❖ Whether or not you are working through an agency (they generally take 25–30 percent off the top)
❖ Your geographical location (some areas of the country pay higher temp wages)
❖ Whether you are in a metropolitan area or in a small town (urban salaries are definitely higher)
❖ Your experience
❖ How aggressive you are in negotiating for "real money"
❖ Your willingness to market yourself
❖ Your willingness to network

Dale Carnegie—the author of classic self-help books such as *How to Win Friends and Influence People*—once said: "About fifteen percent of one's financial success is due to one's technical knowledge, and about eighty-five percent is due to skill in human engineering." Keeping this in mind:

❖ *If you're signed up with a temporary agency, request their highest-paying assignments.* Be confident in your skills and make your experience count. Be "The Temp from Hell." If you're not qualified for the highest-paying work, find out what you have to do to get qualified. Sometimes all it takes is studying a few software manuals and practicing on the computer system at your agency, although more technical jobs may involve advanced coursework. Read the chapter "Market Yourself" on page 21 for more ideas about this.
❖ *Make sure you're being paid a competitive wage for the actual work.* The job description offered by the agency does not always correspond to the responsibilities. For instance, you may be sent to a standard word-processing job, but when you get there you discover that the position also requires spreadsheet work, which pays more. Gladys has several times requested a wage increase when responsibilities increased. She has also volunteered to take on additional work (and additional pay), even though it wasn't part of the original assignment. At the same

time, I have had employers who tried to take advantage of my writing skills within a simple administrative position. I have agreed to do so on the condition that writing time be compensated accordingly or treated as separate freelance work.

❖ *Network! Network! Network!* This can't be emphasized enough. I have "happened upon" freelance writing or graphics projects as an offshoot of a standard office temp job. On one occasion a woman at the next desk knew of someone in another business who was looking for a copywriter. She gave me that person's telephone number, and I subsequently did several assignments for that business.

If you work directly with a company, you can expect a higher hourly salary than if you're connected with an agency. But, when it comes to negotiating salary, how do you know what to ask for?

❖ Check comparative statistics in your field, or contact a professional who would have a sense of the market.
❖ Talk to other people who are doing similar work. You should then be able to determine a reasonable estimate. Be willing to wing it in the beginning, if necessary.
❖ Ask a potential client, "What do you usually pay?" My friend Michael did that at the onset of his freelance photography business, and discovered that "usual pay" was often higher than what he would have requested.

Remember, when working on your own, that you are required to keep track of and pay your own taxes. This means, *don't forget that the tax-person cometh on April 15th*. Once, after several months of a writing assignment, I realized that T-Day was coming up fast and I hadn't adequately prepared for it. How did I cover it? I promptly called my local temporary agency and got an assignment to cover the tax SOS!

Last but not least, Gladys reminds me to mention that "real money" is more visible when it isn't completely swallowed by overhead. This was one of my first hard adjustments when I started temping, as I asked myself the following questions:

❖ Where can I cut back?
❖ Can I survive with less "stuff"?
❖ Can house or car payments, etc., be refinanced to lessen financial burdens?
❖ Can I go easy on credit card purchases?
❖ Is it possible to set aside cash, even if only small amounts?
❖ What high-interest savings plans are available?

Soon after I made some serious cutbacks, I had a discussion with my friend Valerie about it. She agreed that getting along with less stuff was the most difficult part of temporary work. After all, she pointed out, she was in accounting, and money "just came naturally" to her. She likened temping to the time when she backpacked across the country: "I was all over the place and on a limited budget. At first I felt uncertain. Then I realized that I could get along with less. Suddenly having a lot of money didn't seem so important. I felt lighter, more free to concentrate on the sights and experiences."

In temporary work, earning "real money" is a matter of being resourceful, making it happen, and perhaps, as with Valerie, changing your personal definition about what "real money" means. Her statement made sense to me because once I adjusted my idea of how much money I actually needed, I discovered that it is possible to get along with less, and still afford a few luxuries once in a while.

See you at the Ritz.

BENEFITS

R emember health insurance? Paid vacations? How about sick days and holidays? Or retirement plans? I can still imagine them—vaguely. If I squint into the distance, I can see them fluttering on little white wings. And if Gladys reaches on her tiptoes, she can just about spear a holiday with her Temps from Hell pitchfork.

Yes, it's true that you may give up some of the usual benefits when you opt for temping. This need not be as grim as it seems, however, since temporary employment is a transitional situation for most people (ranging from a few weeks to two or three years). Company-sponsored benefits are generally available for the majority of their working life. It is the temping period which is of primary concern for maintaining benefit coverage. There are options.

Temps who are interested in working long-term may qualify for some of these benefits through their agency:

Group medical and hospitalization plans. Many agencies offer programs that you can pay into on a long-term or short-term basis. The requirement is that you must first work for a prescribed number of hours or days. Thirty days is average.

Holiday and vacation pay. Again, these are contingent upon the accrual of a prescribed number of hours. Usually this involves working twelve weeks or more over a four-month period. Or a check equal to one week's salary if you work nine months out of one year. (The catch is that you have to put in the allotted number of hours with *one* agency to get the benefits, which even the hard-working Gladys A. Frumpworth IV can never manage. She once missed Memorial Day pay by thirteen hours!)

Incentive bonuses. Cash bonuses are sometimes available to temps who have received several outstanding reports from clients. Also, the Recommend-a-Friend Program (available through most agencies) offers cash rewards to temps who get a friend to sign up.

Stock-option plans. Some agencies offer their publicly traded stock at a discount rate to temps.

Free skills courses. Classes in computer and administrative skills are available through a number of temporary service offices.

A few agencies offer day-care provision and direct-deposit check systems. Others offer same-week pay. I'm sorry to say that I have so far not heard of an agency awarding paid sick days or retirement plans, although if Gladys catches rumor of something, she'll certainly get her pitchfork out. Hopefully, some enterprising group is cooking up something to that effect even at this moment.

In addition, temporary workers are covered by Workers' Compensation, as required by law. They are also eligible for unemployment insurance benefits, whether they are working through an agency or are on direct contract with a company. The rules for eligibility vary from state to state and are detailed in the Employment Security Act booklet for your state, which is generally available at your local library. Contact your temporary service or state unemployment insurance office for further information.

But you say that you *don't* work through an agency? What benefits are possible? Admittedly, this is a little trickier. In this case, you have to make your own benefits by seeking out alternatives.

Be creative:

❖ Check out group forms of health insurance that are available on an individual basis.

❖ If you have just ended a permanent job, find out if you can remain on the company's insurance program for a period of time. Usually this is an option when you are willing to pay a certain amount on a monthly or quarterly basis.

❖ Write to your senator or representative, stressing the importance of establishing a National Health Care Program that is affordable for all.

❖ If you're married to someone who has a permanent job, you can probably "ride" on his or her medical insurance program. Most health plans for permanent employees include provisions for spouses and dependents.

❖ Open CD or IRA plans at the bank, and research investment in low-risk stocks or money markets in preparation for retirement.

Take a different perspective:

❖ Remember that if your connection with a particular business is direct, you are probably charging a higher hourly rate than you would receive through an agency. This may somewhat balance out the errant perks. Gladys has been known to make *more than twice the amount of money* from working directly with a company rather than going through an agency.

❖ Consider the fact that benefits don't necessarily have to be monetary. For example, flexibility and variety are among the benefits of temping.

This last point is particularly important because agencies report that flexibility and variety are the two main reasons why people do temporary work. Thus, many temps do, in fact, regard them as benefits. Of course, these two qualities won't satisfy the best interests of everyone. In this case, a permanent job will most likely be your safest bet.

WORKING TO YOUR ADVANTAGE

I wrote five children's books during one long-term temporary office assignment. Also, eight short stories, twenty poems, two articles, and a wealth of personal correspondence. I did all this while managing the client's work. *And* the client was pleased.

"What!" you exclaim. "You did all of that? Did your boss know *exactly* what you were doing? How did you get away with it?"

"Of course, the boss knew," I reply. "It was just myself and the telephone, which rang a maximum of fifteen times a day. My boss was away eighty percent of the time on sales calls. I asked several times if there was anything pressing that I might do in his absence. He assured me that there wasn't. 'Just concentrate on taking messages,' he told me. 'Don't worry about anything else.' So, I didn't."

Actually, it's not true that I didn't worry about anything. In the beginning, I felt guilty about doing my own work on company-paid time. I suppose I had some residual fear about being caught passing notes in the fifth grade. Or part of me expected the detention hall monitor to appear out of nowhere, tap my hand with a ruler, and make me write "I will do my homework" 100 times on the blackboard. I was concerned about obeying the American Work Ethic, which I translated as the importance of working hard, even if this meant busy work. Even if the work was in no way productive.

This was before Gladys A. Frumpworth IV had a little chat with me about the matter.

"What are you waiting for?" she said one day, after the boss left on a week-long sales trip and the phone hadn't rung for three hours.

I was straightening the already straight office supply closet, and her booming voice startled me so that I jumped about a foot. Gladys loomed ten feet over my head, with her hands on her hips, and fireworks sparking out of her green eyes. Her screaming-red hair looked like a wild tornado about her head.

"This is the perfect opportunity for you to write," she continued. "You would rather waste your time doing busy work?"

I didn't know Gladys very well at this point, and I found her a little intimidating.

"Well, no," I stammered. "But—"

I turned back to the closet and concentrated on the rows of little sticky notes, making sure that they were in perfect lines.

"But, *what*?" she growled. "Allow me to point out the reality of the situation. You have nothing to do for the job. You have been given permission to do what you like. You have plenty of writing to do. What are you waiting for? Get going! I'll watch the telephones."

So, beneath Gladys's loving glare, I went to work. I learned a new graphics package, which enabled me not only to write my books but to execute the illustrations as well. Meanwhile, Gladys gave A+ attention to clients on the telephone and mailed company literature to prospective customers. By the end of the assignment, I had enhanced my writing career *and* my boss was satisfied that his business had grown. (In fact, he requested me again the following year.) As we shook hands and I walked out the door, I felt a sense of accomplishment for us both. Then I felt something warm on my shoulder. When I turned around, I saw that it was Gladys giving me a reassuring pat. She was too polite to say, "I told you so," but I understood that we would be temping partners from then on.

If there is nothing pressing on an assignment, make the time yours. Especially if no one is breathing down your neck and expecting you to look busy. You probably have your own list, but here are some ideas:

❖ *Teach yourself about equipment or computer sofware.* It will enhance your chances of a wider variety of jobs in the future. Also, it might open up new prospects for a career that you never dreamed of.

❖ *Read the office literature.* There might be something of interest. Also, it will make you more knowledgeable about the company if someone asks.

❖ *Take advantage of classes or programs offered through the company.* Sometimes large companies have ongoing in-house programs in computer skills or interpersonal skills. The same businesses often have fitness centers with exercise equipment, weight rooms, or aerobics classes for the employees.

❖ *Job-hunt.* If you're looking for permanent work, a temporary situation can offer the time and equipment for sprucing up your résumé, making copies, and making telephone contacts. A temp correspondent in Seattle reported that she spent a six-week assignment doing nothing but answering telephones and applying for permanent positions. By the end of the six weeks, she had a job.

❖ *Take the time to learn a new subject.* Go to the library during lunch and take out books on whatever looks interesting. I began a study of Chinese herbal medicine during one assignment. My friend Jerome used one long-term job to conduct his own "survey course" on art history.

❖ *Work on a personal project.* Write a book. Write a letter to your parents. Address envelopes as a volunteer assignment for your local charity. Knit a sweater. Send your Christmas cards. You'll appreciate the time to do something else when you get home.

❖ *Enjoy doing nothing.* Sometimes doing nothing in particular is exactly the prescription we need. Sitting back, staring into space or out the window, and concentrating on just breathing can be an oasis in the day.

❖ *Do temporary work while traveling.* Agencies abound in every city, making it possible to work and pay for the trip at the same time. I know several temps who have traveled extensively, doing temporary work, and seeing the sights along the way.

Do all of these things. Or do the things from your personal list. Do them while successfully managing the daily work load. By the time you get home, you'll feel that you've had a productive day—while being paid! There are many advantages to temping. Make them work for you.

SHORT-TERM OR LONG-TERM?

I always thought that "short-term" and "long-term" were straightforward until I started temping. That is, they weren't issues that I paid much attention to at all. So when I first came across short-term and long-term assignments, I thought, what's the big deal? Wasn't short-term *short*? Wasn't long-term *long*? We-ell, maybe not exactly, I considered after giving it some thought. How short was a short-term assignment? How long was a long-term assignment? At this point I got confused. Fortunately, Gladys was able to enlighten me with her unique brand of mind-boggling logic.

"Time is relative," she pronounced. "You'll have your own definition when you've had a few long- and short-term assignments of your own. Then you'll be able to compare the two."

Gladys cut a Granny Smith apple into eighths, offered me a piece, and took one for herself.

I chewed my piece of apple while thinking about what she said. I chewed the apple completely. I chewed the thought completely. By the time I swallowed both apple and thought, long- and short-term still didn't make sense.

Gladys could see that I didn't understand. "Okay," she said. "Let's be totally ridiculous. Let's say you're offered two assignments—one that is a minute long and one that is a century long. Which one is short-term and which one is long-term?"

"That *is* ridiculous," I agreed. "Of course, one minute is short-term, and one century is long-term."

"Good," she said. "You basically understand. Now suppose you're offered two more assignments. One is one minute long and one is thirty seconds long."

I replied without hesitation. "They're both short-term."

"But compared with each other?"

"Oh." I frowned. "I see what you mean."

Despite herself, Gladys chuckled, but she was willing to offer the following guidelines.

In the temp business a short-term assignment ranges from one day to two or three weeks. These generally cover a particular job while a regular employee is on vacation or sick leave.

Long-term positions involve a few weeks to a year, or more. They include situations in which (a) an employee is on extended leave of absence, such as maternity or disability; (b) an employee has left the company and a suitable replacement is being sought; (c) the position is fulfilling a specific contract period; (d) the position is functioning as a probation period prior to a full-time offer; and (e) the position is designed to function only to be filled by temporary personnel.

Whether the assignment is short-term or long-term, there are advantages and disadvantages to both:

ADVANTAGES OF SHORT-TERM TEMPORARY ASSIGNMENTS

❖ Frequent turnover. Some temps report that constant change keeps them from being bored.

❖ Not being locked in for an indefinite period if you don't feel compatible with an assignment. Gladys once worked at a company that tests explosives. She was grateful to leave after a few days.

❖ "Quick fix" cash without a long-term commitment. My friend Tina, whose main source of income is her translation work, often takes one- or two-day assignments specifically to pay for something special, such as buying a new pair of shoes or going out to dinner.

DISADVANTAGES OF SHORT-TERM ASSIGNMENTS

❖ Inadequate time to digest the assignment or company. Especially if it's a place that you might like to go permanent with.

❖ Stress of more frequent transitions. I knew a receptionist who temped at a different company every day for two weeks, and reported that she felt like a "human yo-yo."

ADVANTAGES OF LONG-TERM ASSIGNMENTS

❖ Fewer transitions

❖ More flexibility to negotiate a change of hours, higher pay, a day off, etc.

❖ Opportunity to develop rapport

❖ Regular cash-flow

❖ Time to perfect a skill, such as a new software package, which may prove useful in future assignments

❖ Time to accrue enough hours to be eligible for holiday and/or vacation benefits through an agency

DISADVANTAGES OF LONG-TERM ASSIGNMENTS

❖ Emulation of a "permanent" job in terms of responsibility, but without the benefits

❖ Boredom. The job becomes routine. One long-term temp confided that she felt co-workers took her for granted but didn't accept her as part of the company—as she put it, "the worst of both worlds."

As Gladys predicted, after working temporary for a year or more, my idea about short-term and long-term changed. At the advent of my temporary reign, a three-day assignment made me nervous because I couldn't predict beyond that point. Would I get another job? Would I survive financially? Would the transition be stressful? Now I am more comfortable with a commitment of two weeks to two months. This gives me the benefit of getting to know the company, of settling in a bit, while stopping short of becoming too routine.

To add confusion to the issue, it isn't always clear at the beginning when a position is long-term or short-term. For example, a client might bill a job as being short-term when, in fact, the assignment is indefinite. I have worked with clients who wanted to assess me before officially committing to a longer time period, and clients who expected to fill a position more quickly than they were able. Other companies have been pleased enough with my work to delay their search for a permanent employee. Conversely, assignments that are labeled "indefinite" may run considerably shorter because a full-time employee is hired sooner than the employer expected, or an assigned temp doesn't match the requirements of the job. So you can't always tell.

This reminds me of my friend Tom, who began a temporary career in electronics and was baffled by this same issue of short-term versus long-term. The first person Tom met on the job was a professional temp, who traveled from state to state, finding production work wherever she went. When she asked Tom how long he would be there and he told her six weeks, she replied, "Oh, now you'll be stable for a while."

"She calls six weeks 'stable'?" he told me on the phone that night. "Six *weeks*? I don't get it!"

As he rambled on, sounding more amazed with each sentence, I felt myself smiling.

"Time is relative," I said in my Gladys voice. "You'll have a better sense of this when you've had a few more assignments. Wait and see."

Which proved prophecy when his assignment surpassed the six-month mark.

WORKING ON SHORT NOTICE

Ah, it's the life. You are sitting in your sunny-morning kitchen, sipping a mug of freshly ground coffee with honey and cream, and munching on cinnamon toast. Your favorite music is on the radio. Your cat is purring in your lap. Needless to say, you're still in your bathrobe and fuzzy bunny slippers—after all, you weren't planning to go out. You have a whole day to look forward to. A whole luxurious day to yourself. You've even given your alter ego—the one who does temp work—the day off. You'll have a second cup of coffee. Maybe go for a long walk. Maybe write some poetry. The possibilities are endless. You begin to make a list when the telephone rings.

Just in case it's a literary magazine saying that they are pleased to publish your latest set of poems, or the lottery commission congratulating you on your million-dollar win, you quickly grab the receiver. But the voice on the other end isn't what you expected.

"Hello! This is Temptation Temporary Service. We have a job that we think might interest you. Are you available?"

"We-ell—" you begin.

"It starts this morning. Can you get there in half an hour?"

Your eyes trace an isosceles triangle from your fur-covered bathrobe to the pad of paper to a sudden mental image of your checkbook in the next room. The checkbook has been on a diet for a while, but it's not starving. Your thoughts scramble over one hundred options in a single second, as every excuse ever made rushes to your head. You feel your legs grow a deep Gumby-green. Yes, they are bending and twisting at the knees. Maybe you should take the job, you think. Maybe this luxurious day wasn't meant to be. You hear yourself about to give in to Temptation, but your answer seems to be tangled up in your vocal cords. Meanwhile, the voice on the other end doesn't know that a century just passed.

"Are you still there?" Temptation is saying. "Here, let me give you the details."

And, as the details are revealed, you are faced with the moment of truth that is familiar to every temp: *just how flexible are you?*

Do you: (a) strrrrrrr-etch and bend your way to the job because the state of your checkbook has dipped below the poverty level? (b) Grab up this excellent opportunity because over a thousand other temps may be vying for this job, and you don't want to muff your chances? (c) Resist Temptation because your poetry mind is going strong, and the income isn't worth giving up a potential Nobel Prize?

Of course, your decision depends on how low your bank account *actually* is, how close to the Nobel Prize you *actually* are, and how quickly you adapt to transition. It also depends on how long you've been doing temporary work. This is important because experience speaks. Experience tells you how much you are risking if you turn down a position, and gives you an idea of how flexible you should necessarily be. Also, the longer you work temporary, the more knowledge you accrue. The advantage to this is that you can choose from a greater variety of jobs; you are risking very little if you turn one down.

When I began temping, I was 90 percent Gumby. After all, I was green to the temporary world. I wasn't sure how flexible I needed to be to keep up with the flow, so I was superflexible. Bend-over-backward flexible. The agency knew they could count on me to take whatever they offered. I was busy all the time.

After a year or two, I eased up. I switched agencies, and declined jobs that weren't appealing. Which didn't in any way alter my options. While the new agency soon discovered that I wasn't bound to accept every assignment, they realized that I could always be relied upon to give them my best.

When you work temporary, the telephone can ring at any time. Availability is what the temping game is all about. But you may be able to balance out an awkward moment of truth by:

❖ Informing your agency in advance that you prefer at least a day of notice for an assignment
❖ Informing your agency when you will be unavailable for long periods of time
❖ Making a firm decision in your own mind—yes or no—before the telephone rings

❖ Being gracious about saying no. Be apologetic and ask the agency to please call again. Let them know that you are still interested.

❖ Letting your answering machine take a message. You can return the call later in the day, or when you are available.

❖ Preparing yourself physically and emotionally in advance if you do wish to work

❖ Having clothing ready for a possible assignment. Not being involved in a difficult-to-interrupt project can make a last-minute work assignment less hectic.

Whether you accept short-notice assignments is a personal decision. Some people are more flexible than others. Because I work better with a little notice, I generally try not to put myself in the position of making on-the-spot decisions. And because temping can be so erratic, I strive to structure the rest of my life as best I can. This means that if I'm working at home, I give Gladys A. Frumpworth IV a well-deserved day off and try to stay with my plan for writing poetry (or cleaning the house, or walking, or whatever)—unless, of course, the assignment is something that is too good to turn down. Otherwise, I let the answering machine take the call and touch base with the agency later in the day.

Sure, I take the risk of losing the job by waiting, but if I can afford it, that's okay. I know that there *will* be another job, that I haven't turned down the last money-making proposition to ever hit earth. I also know how flexible I need to be—that it isn't necessary to get too bent out of shape. So when the telephone rings, I snuggle up in my robe and bunny slippers and pour that second cup of coffee. Pass the cinnamon toast, please.

DO TEMPS HAVE A BAD IMAGE?

My friend Ben does temporary office jobs to support his free-lance art business. He doesn't say a lot about himself at work, just concentrates on being thorough and friendly. He enjoys his assignments for several months, until he finds himself working for someone who treats him differently. Instead of assigning him interesting tasks, she gives him menial work. Instead of returning Ben's cheerful "Good morning," she smiles at another co-worker and chats with *her*. She refers to Ben, not by name, but as "the temp."

One day, she sees him working on an art project at lunch. She asks about it, and he explains. Suddenly her attitude toward him seems to change. He begins to receive more challenging projects. She not only says, "Good morning, Ben," but strikes up conversations throughout the day. Why? Ben wonders. Certainly he is the same person as he was at the beginning of the assignment. He is puzzled, until he realizes that, in this woman's mind, he now has a real identity. He is "an artist." He is no longer just "the temp."

Although it doesn't happen on every job, there comes a time in every temp's career when we realize that temps sometimes have a bad image. When I heard Ben's story, I invited him to a Temps from Hell meeting to hear what ideas Gladys had on the subject. Gladys can recognize what she calls "tempist" attitudes the minute she walks in the door of an assignment. She explains that such bad images occur largely because employers and permanent workers don't understand the temporary lifestyle. Who is this person? they wonder. Why doesn't he have a real job? What does he want out of this situation? They simply don't comprehend the concept of being temporary, especially when it is the temp's choice. Because . . .

❖ Employers or co-workers don't trust someone they don't know.
❖ Companies don't trust someone who is just passing through.
❖ Permanent workers assume that a person does temporary work because he is unskilled or incompetent, that he can't get a "real job," or was fired from his last work situation.

❖ Co-workers suspect that the temp might want their jobs. This is particularly true in a company that is undergoing staff cuts.

❖ People don't think. It doesn't occur to them when they exclude temps from a situation that it might be hurtful, because they have never temped themselves and they can't relate to the feeling.

❖ If a company has a strong hierarchy, temps are viewed as being at the bottom of the totem pole as part of the natural progression.

❖ If a business environment is tense, people may be jealous because the temp can just walk away whenever he or she wants. Unfortunately, it may feel safer to vent bad feelings on a temp than on permanent co-workers, who more directly affect their job security.

If a company or individual has a bad image of temps, it will be apparent in many ways. For example, when people explain procedures, they are condescending or oversimplifying. . . . A simple project comes up that you aren't allowed to do because it might be too involved for a temp. . . . You hear frequent stories about previous temps, *all* of whom were incompetent. . . . The temp is suspected of taking missing office supplies. . . . No one wants to take responsibility for a project that has gone wrong, so the temp is blamed. . . . The office has a party and you aren't invited because you aren't a permanent employee. . . .

By offering these lists, I don't mean to encourage temporary workers to become paranoid in their everyday dealings on the job. I only emphasize that if any of the above scenarios occur regularly, you need to be aware that the company involved has a bad image of temps, and you will need to protect yourself. I have experienced all of the above, but the situations were mostly clumped within only four or five out of the more than one hundred companies I have worked for. The most logical explanation I can derive from this is that bad attitudes about temporary workers are generated from the top and spread throughout the rest of the employees.

While such attitudes are no fun, they can sometimes be counteracted and, actually, reversed, as Gladys discovered after much experimentation with the subject. When her experiments were concluded, she barricaded herself in her office for several weeks as she analyzed each situation. Finally, she called a Temps from Hell meeting, served up hot chocolate with peppermint sticks and whipped cream, and revealed how temps can counteract bad images:

❖ Confidently jump into a situation and assure people that you can do the work.

❖ Be open and let people get to know you. Don't count on co-workers to begin conversations. Let them know from the beginning that you aren't interested in their jobs, but you do enjoy getting to know people. Believe it or not, permanent employees frequently have the idea that temps don't want to talk, that they don't want to be part of the situation.

❖ Ask questions.

❖ Politely inform people when lengthy explanations for simple procedures are unnecessary.

❖ Show your résumé to employers (you can explain that you're not applying for the job and that this is only for their information). Offering a list of your background and skills often sets people at ease.

❖ Recognize when a company attitude seems "tempist" but isn't. This is often the case with government contractors, who are strictly regulated. Such companies generally require temps to fill out nondisclosure agreements and sign in and out of the building. In extreme cases, temps may not be allowed anywhere in the building without supervision. Also, when a company is large, permanent employees may not realize when a temporary worker steps on board. They may assume that temps are permanent employees from another department.

❖ Don't contribute to the problem. Please don't make personal phone calls all day, or type your grocery list when there is work to be done. This kind of attitude pins a bad image on all temporary workers who follow you.

But suppose that you find yourself up against a "tempist" environment, even if you have scrupulously followed these steps. In this case, don't be combative or spend several hours a day crying in the bathroom, as Gladys did on one month-long assignment that she now calls the "red-eyed job." Instead, dry your eyes, look for another assignment, and try not to take it personally. Remember that employers don't know you well enough to be personal in their attitudes.

In the event that you decide to tackle a negative environment, admit its existence, then work around it. Remind yourself that, as a temp, you don't have to go along with a bad image. Do your job as quietly, professionally, and conscientiously as possible. Continue to be pleasant to people, to expose companies to the fact that temps can be competent, intelligent, and congenial workers. After her red-eyed assignment, Gladys found that being a cheerful hellion often catches on, that such an attitude "grows on people." You never know when your positive influence will be contagious and change someone's mind.

ON THE JOB

THE FIRST DAY

One of my first temporary jobs was when I was twelve. The employers were the parents of five boys, ages two to ten. My mission was to arrive just after dinner, give baths to the youngest two, make sure that all of them brushed their teeth, wrestle the youngest four into bed by 9:00 P.M., and see that the eldest didn't watch too much television. Did I succeed? Well, let's just say I did my best. By the time the parents arrived home at eleven, three boys had brushed their teeth, two were asleep, one had watched television nonstop, one had cut off the feet of his new bunny pajamas, and I had managed to mop up all three inches of water from the bathroom floor. Not bad for a first day!

Much of temp work is taking care of something: caring for someone else's job while they're on vacation . . . caring for an employer who is looking for a permanent employee . . . giving TLC to a pet project. Whatever the job, something or someone is entrusted to your care for a short time. Your assignment is to carefully nurture that work, whether it is doing technical drawings or answering telephones. Once you figure out what it is that has to be taken care of, the rest will fall into place. But probably not on the first day.

First days can be intimidating. Mostly because we don't know what to expect. As a temp, I've had one hundred first days, and I still face them with a certain amount of trepidation. In fact, on my last first day, I reread this chapter to remind myself what to do.

I've had first days where everything has gone so smoothly that I hardly noticed them, and ones where every machine in the place broke down at the sight of me and I called everyone by the wrong name. I've had first days that were last days (also known as one-day assignments). By their very nature, first days are challenging.

The only way to survive is to Just Do It, Go Through It, and prepare yourself as much as possible.

❖ Don't have too many expectations and don't be too hard on
yourself if the first day isn't perfect. Everything will fall into
place later.

❖ Wear something that you feel especially good about. You'll do
better if you feel comfortable with your appearance.

❖ Eat breakfast, even if it's just a piece of toast. You'll need the
energy. And unless you're immune to the effects of coffee, skip
a second cup. The Temp from Hell (who has a naturally caffein-
ated personality) takes this one step further and sticks with
herbal tea on first days.

❖ Take lunch. Some companies have vending machines or even
full-service cafeterias, but you can't count on it. There may not
be a restaurant or deli near the work site, either.

❖ Give yourself something to look forward to when the day is
over. A planned dinner with a friend or a walk around the lake
can provide a psychological "dessert" for getting through the
day.

❖ Plan to arrive at the assignment a few minutes early. You'll be
less nervous if you don't have to rush around.

❖ Make a good first impression. According to experienced speech-
makers, it only takes twelve words or fifteen seconds to make a
first impression. A smile and a handshake can successfully give
a first impression within that time frame. A positive beginning
paves the way for a positive assignment.

❖ Pay attention to your own first impressions of people on the job.
These usually tell you what you can expect throughout the assignment, so allow your nervousness to take a back seat and
concentrate on how co-workers act. Handshakes, facial expres-
sions, and general body language are important clues. For example, Gladys once worked for three people at a certain
company. The first person was elusive for the first two days. The
second remained at her desk and smiled briefly when Gladys
was introduced at her office door. The third rose from his chair,
walked across the room, shook her hand, and said, "Welcome

aboard!'' Guess who she got along with best? These patterns of action held true for the duration of the assignment.

❖ Ask questions and write down the answers. It will be easier to sort everything out on subsequent days.

❖ Remember that it's the first day for the clients, too. You're new to them, and they don't know what to expect either.

As usual, of course, have a sense of humor. Gladys tells me this time and time again, and she is right—especially when applied to unsuccessful first days. "Every situation has the potential of a funny story, to be appreciated later" is one of her famous mottoes.

One such story involves my eager-to-please friend Valerie on her first day of a paralegal assignment. She attacked the files with such vigor that she somehow managed to pull out two drawers at once, toppling the entire cabinet and its contents onto the floor. Fortunately, nothing but Valerie's pride was injured, but the rest of the day involved uprighting the cabinet and sorting out the folders, which required the aid of her disgruntled supervisor. A similar incident is my one-day-long waitressing "career" of many years ago, when I accidentally dumped a whole tray of Bloody Marys onto someone's white linen lap. Oops!

It's not surprising that Valerie wasn't invited back for a second day at the law office, nor that I was promptly liberated from waitress duty, despite profuse apologies on both of our parts. However, we somehow recovered, lived on to laugh at ourselves, and survived many more first days. And, as we later asked ourselves at a Temps from Hell meeting: Aren't cabinets supposed to have safety catches that prevent more than one drawer being opened at once? And aren't people who drink Bloody Marys required to wear *red*?

COMMUNICATION DO'S AND DON'TS

O ne of my temporary stints was at a toy store during Christmas season. My job was to walk the floor with a puppet on my hand, amusing children while their parents shopped. I became thoroughly acquainted with the zoo of puppets on the shelves and soon perfected my frog voice, my snake wiggle, my wolf howl, and my fox trot. I made the gorilla puppet sing and dance. The children loved it and followed me around the store like I was the Pied Piper. I felt tired but gratified when I went home at five o'clock.

After several weeks, my hours changed. The schedule was posted and, under my name, it said "In: noon, Out: 8:00 P.M." I arrived promptly at noon on the first day, and went to work. Likewise, when eight o'clock arrived, I headed for the door. I was halfway to my car when I heard the manager calling my name.

"Where are you going?" she wanted to know.

"Home," I replied. "Wasn't I scheduled from noon to eight?"

"Yes," returned the manager. "But those are your hours to *work with customers*. From eight to eight-thirty, you have to vacuum the store."

I wanted to know if I got paid for vacuuming the store.

"Of course. Why do you ask?"

"Since that time isn't on the schedule, it looks like I don't work during that time period."

At this point, the manager seemed to stop listening, and I saw that she was staring at my arm. I then realized that the gorilla was still on my hand, and I was making the puppet's mouth move as I talked!

After we shared a good laugh, the manager wrote up the schedule for my actual hours, and I agreed to vacuum. We both resolved to maintain *direct* communication from then on.

I am now many assignments past those toy store days, and I think I have learned to communicate effectively without a puppet on my hand, although I try to remember that communication is an ongoing learning process. As always, it doesn't hurt to have a few guidelines. Here are a few communication do's.

GET INFORMATION UP FRONT. If the job is through an agency, get as much information as possible about an assignment before arriving at the work site—company name, the nature of the business, directions, full name of the contact person, wages, hours, length of assignment, dress requirements (if applicable), and responsibilities. If you are working directly with the client, make sure that you agree on a payment schedule, hours, and deadlines before beginning the project.

REMEMBER THAT COMMUNICATION BEGINS DURING THE FIRST SECOND OF A JOB. Smiles, direct eye contact, and handshakes establish open communication at the onset of an assignment. Introduce yourself to people who aren't introduced to you. Ask necessary questions.

ESTABLISH RAPPORT. As elementary as it may seem, simple courtesies like "Good morning," "How are you?," "Please," "Thank you," "Good night," and "Have a good weekend" encourage people to connect. Make brief and pleasant conversation. Compliment people whenever you can sincerely do so. ("What an exquisite tarantula tie!")

MAINTAIN COMMUNICATION ON A DAILY BASIS. Apprise the clients of your progress on projects and ask for help, if necessary, on prioritizing. Find out answers to questions that you don't know. If you suspect that there is a misunderstanding about something, clear it up before it escalates. Let people know when you are taking breaks or going to lunch. (Gladys usually says, "Ciao!")

COMMUNICATE WITH YOURSELF. Admit when a particular assignment or company isn't right for you, and take the necessary steps to change it. Listen to your intuition. I can usually tell within a day or two if a job isn't going to work out. It's better to act on your feelings in the beginning than to regret it later.

INFORM EMPLOYERS (AND/OR THE TEMPORARY AGENCY) OF YOUR AVAILABILITY. Give your supervisor a few days of warning when you have a dental appointment or a job interview; then remind her again on the day of the appointment. If you need to take a day off, ask whether the client needs a replacement for that time. Try to give a few days' notice to both the client and agency if for any reason you decide that you need to leave an assignment before its term is over.

COMMUNICATE NONVERBALLY. Smiles, waves, nods, and brief notes via paper or electronic mail can make a difference in someone's day. Gladys is fond of scribbling "Hi!" or a funny message on tiny yellow notes and secretly sticking them to her co-worker's desks.

LEAVE A BRIEF STATUS REPORT ON THE LAST DAY. The next person (or the returning person) and employers will appreciate the update. Also, tell people you are leaving so that they will be aware of the transition.

WHEN IT'S APPROPRIATE, CONTINUE COMMUNICATION *AFTER* THE ASSIGNMENT IS OVER. If you are particularly pleased with a person or company, why not write a letter of thanks? I have done this on several occasions. It not only makes people feel good, but offers a long-lasting impression that may lead to future assignments.

What about communication don'ts? Although we don't like to emphasize negativity, there are a few issues to avoid.

DON'T ALLOW NEGATIVE ATTITUDES TO PERSIST. While it's human to be in a bad mood once in a while, negative attitudes should be stopped before they get the best of you. Try to acknowledge a bad attitude, determine its cause, and deal with it by either working with the problem or getting past it. A bad attitude may be signaling something as simple as the need for a break. A day off in the middle of a long-term assignment can be an emotional oasis. (The Temp from Hell uses this approach with great success.) Or a bad attitude may be telling you that you need to leave the job altogether.

DON'T FORGET TO CALL EITHER THE AGENCY OR THE CLIENT WHEN YOU'RE SICK. In fact, call *two* people at the job. I once left a message on an employer's voice mail, only to discover the next day that he was also out, had left a message on *my* voice mail, and no one knew where either one of us was.

DON'T SHOW A STRONG DISLIKE FOR AN INDIVID-UAL OR COMPANY. Someone may be difficult to work with, but it isn't worth dwelling on in a temporary assignment. Try to be as pleasant as possible, and remember that you will soon be moving on. If your dislike is for the business itself (e.g., if you don't agree with its philosophy or you don't like the way the boss talks to her employees), perhaps this indicates that you should find a business you feel more compatible with. Gladys once quit a lucrative résumé-writing job when she discovered that the clients were being badly treated.

DON'T GOSSIP. One of the advantages of being a temp is a built-in distance from office politics. Co-workers may choose to confide in you because they feel safer talking to someone who is outside of the situation and who will soon be leaving. Listen if you think it will ease someone's mind, but your job will be much simpler if you don't get involved in tale-telling or side-taking.

DON'T BURN BRIDGES. Try not to leave a job on a sour note. A situation may be unpleasant, but you'll be amazed at how quickly the unpleasantness wears off when the assignment is over. I heard about one temp who was so unhappy that she left a long note chastising the business, as well as certain individuals in her department. The upshot was that the note was forwarded to her temporary agency, which terminated her without warning. Losing that contact wasn't worth burning bridges over.

In summary, whatever the nature of the assignment, temporary work runs more smoothly and is more pleasant when you communicate as openly as possible with everyone, including yourself. After a while, it becomes a matter of habit. With or without a gorilla puppet on your hand.

DRESS CODES

We've worked with dress codes, and we've worked without them. We've worked around them and threaded through them. Generally, if we get our hands on a written copy of a company's costuming no-nos, most are items that we would never consider wearing to a business in the first place—for instance, when was the last time you saw someone sitting at her desk in a *bathing* suit?

For the most part, unless we work for a financial company, slick advertising agency, law firm, or similar high-profile business, whatever clean, professional clothes we have are fine. The main thing is to get the requirements up front. The jargon is as follows:

❖ Professional Dress: Formal skirt, or pants and blouse or jacket for women, and nice pants (no jeans) and button-down shirt (possibly a tie) for men. Shoes for both men and women should be tidy, e.g., polished loafers, flats, or heels. Definitely no running shoes.

❖ Casual Dress: "Good" or designer jeans (no faded, tie-dyed, or torn, please), informal skirt, blouse, or sport shirt—a blend-in-with-the-walls, won't-offend-anybody sort of outfit. Sneakers may be acceptable if they are clean and in good shape.

❖ Anything Goes: As it sounds, and probably means that you're headed for a very low-key environment or a messy job.

While it's a good idea to dress according to the jargon on the first day, what it really gets down to is what you see with your own eyes: the really-o, truly-o, *in practice* dress code. After that, it's easy. Just pay attention to the atmosphere of the business, then dress to fit in.

This reminds me of a software design company that I temped at, where the standard uniform was faded blue jeans, T-shirts ablaze with interesting sayings, and sneakers that looked like they had snuck over from the Black Lagoon. Everyone dressed this way, the president included. Taking their cue, I jumped on the anything-goes band wagon. Then one day I discovered an employee hand-book, and guess what? The dress code strictly forbade the very things that everyone wore!

A reverse situation involved a short stint at a bank, my only occasion as a temp for which a skirt was actually required. Uh-oh time. After diving head-first into my closet, I finally came up with a *split* skirt. Maybe if I held my legs firmly together, no one would notice. Let's see, I calculated, the job was for two weeks. Did I have enough alternating tops/jackets to see that split skirt through? In a pinch, would harem pants do? Or worse, on my limited budget, would I have to go shopping for a skirt? A second minor panic set in. Thankfully, it turned out to be a false alarm. The next morning I was greeted at the job site by my supervisor, who was not only wearing pants, but *tight* ones. I coasted through the job on my existing wardrobe with no problem.

Feeling confused after these experiences, I asked Gladys A. Frumpworth IV to address the rules concerning dress codes. As a temp, was I really expected to dress up? I asked. Did businesses understand that temporary workers often live on restricted funds? Did they care? Were dress codes really arbitrary, after all?

I wanted some real answers, but Gladys merely winked as she walked by in a striking outfit that included a sequined beret, a leopard scarf, and striped socks. Clearly, *she* didn't take this dress code stuff too seriously. So I spoke with the manager of a temporary agency in Boston instead.

"Professional dress requirements are pretty standard for professional work, whether you're a permanent employee or a temp, but it's possible to dress nicely without spending a lot of money," she told me, lowering her voice to mention a certain bargain basement store. "Generally, people are going to be too busy working to read the labels on your clothes. Of course, if you're looking for a permanent job, you might want to go all out," she added, handing me her typical dress code list.

A woman's basic wardrobe might include:

❖ One or two solid-colored skirts
❖ Solid-colored shoes to coordinate with the skirts

❖ A variety of blouses and/or jackets
❖ Plenty of accessories such as belts and scarves

A man's basic wardrobe consists of:

❖ One or two pairs of nice slacks
❖ A jacket or two to coordinate with the slacks
❖ A pair of "nice" shoes
❖ Solid-colored shirts
❖ A few ties

"How you dress isn't nearly as important as attitude," the manager said, after I had skimmed the list. "If you have a great smile and you dress as yourself, chances are that you're going to be better at what you do. Within reason, of course," she added as her eye was caught by a woman coming through the door in torn blue jeans.

"I have one temp who is into purple," she continued. "I mean, *really* into purple. Even her hair has a slight tint. She doesn't dress straight-office, but she's one of our best workers. So I send her to the more open-atmosphere places, and when I call a client I say 'I hope you like purple.' "

As you might suspect, this woman was a bit on the artistic side herself. When our interview was over, she suddenly leaned across the desk and grabbed my wrist. "I *adore* Minnie!" she exclaimed, looking at my watch. She held up her own watch—a Mickey Mouse that talked—and waved at a woman in sequined beret, leopard scarf, and striped socks who was walking past the window.

PRIORITIZING

I can happily work for ten uninterrupted hours on a writing project, but when I'm handed a double-sided copying job, a hundred pages, ten copies, I go to pieces. Especially when someone says, "Hey, can you grab that phone?" *and* "I need these letters typed," *and* "Would you look in the files for this folder, please?" *and* "These time sheets need to be filled out right away" *and* the list continues until it equals a stack the size of the Empire State Building. Top it off with an impatient somebody pacing in front of the desk, glaring at his watch, and I'm ready for a multiple task breakdown.

This is when I SOS for Gladys.

Wonder temp that she is, she rushes to my anguished cry and begins to direct traffic. With her whistle in her mouth and her red hair looking like a stop light, she skillfully moves everything into manageable stacks. With her hand up, she discourages new projects from coming in. Then she sits by my side and holds my hand.

"Breathe!" she commands. "Take a deep breath! Now take another one."

After five minutes of impromptu meditation, she brings me a nice cup of herbal tea and pats my hand. "Doesn't this feel better?" she asks.

I nod.

"Good," she says. "Now you're ready to learn to prioritize."

"Okay," I say.

"I happen to have a little something typed up, just for the occasion," Gladys assures me. She shuffles through a stack of papers and pulls out a single sheet. The lesson begins.

PRIORITIZING MULTIPLE TASKS
by Gladys A. Frumpworth IV

1. Assess the tasks at hand and determine which is most important. If you're not sure, ask. Find out which projects can be moved to another day if necessary.

2. Organize the tasks into manageable stacks, in order of importance. Don't worry about how long this takes. You'll work more efficiently once you're organized. Number the stacks if you have to, using sticky notes, so that you won't have to think about the order later.

3. Don't distract yourself with unnecessary papers. Dispose of all memos and reminders when you no longer need them. This applies particularly to small pieces of scrap paper and past-their-prime sticky notes. File correspondence and copies *now* instead of later. Uncluttered desk, uncluttered mind.

4. Approach the stacks one by one. Pay complete attention to each stack and do the work as thoroughly and conscientiously as possible. Take whatever time is necessary to complete it. Don't worry about the next project. Don't forget to breathe. As soon as the work is completed to your satisfaction, set it aside and out of sight. ("Out of sight, out of mind.")

5. Ask for help if necessary. When you suspect that you can't finish a project in time, avoid a last-minute panic by asking for assistance or seeing if the deadline can be extended.

6. Keep an in-box open for additional new projects. Process these projects when you have a break from your current tasks. If someone has something that requires explanation, ask if it can wait a few minutes until you come to a reasonable stopping point. Or set up a specific time later in the day to discuss the details.

7. Expect the telephone to ring at the most critical moment. This is par for the course, so you may as well *plan* for it to happen. No use pulling your hair out over spilt milk, or crying over lost hair, or however that saying goes. Make sure a memo pad and pen are by the phone so you don't have to interrupt yourself by searching for them. If the telephone rings more in the morning, try to save focused projects for the afternoon. Of course, if possible, ask someone else to watch the phones, or switch on the answering machine when a large project is at hand.

8. Take breaks. Have a cup of tea. Read a poem. Meditate. Look at a scenic picture. Go for a short walk. Sometimes getting

away from a project gives you perspective and helps the schedule run more smoothly.

9. Take a minute to visualize the light at the end of the tunnel. If you find yourself in a panic, force yourself to stop and close your eyes. Breathe deeply. As you breathe, imagine the stacks of work gradually disappearing until your desk is clear. Watch yourself sigh with relief and accomplishment. Visualize the end of the day when you are finished and on your way out the door. Now, quick! Take advantage of that calm feeling and get back to work!

10. Remember that there are only eight hours in a workday (usually). Just because the stacks reach the ceiling, it doesn't mean that it's possible or necessary to finish everything today. Working steadily and methodically is the best that anyone can do. If this isn't enough, it may be best to cross your fingers and believe in tomorrow.

Even with a copy of Gladys's steps in front of me, I still find that multiple tasks are a stress factor on the job. And I don't think that I'm alone. I have found that it helps to admit that I am easily upset by multiple tasks before an upset appears. This gives co-workers a chance to plan ahead and be sensitive in their demands. Like the darling man who understood my panic over multiple tasks and devised a strategy. He warned me first thing in the morning when he had an upcoming project. After it was in my hands, he checked in at reasonable intervals to see how I was doing and whether there was anything he could do to help. (Make photocopies? No problem. Get more printer paper from the supply room? At your service.) When everything was finished, he thanked me for my contribution. Because of his thoughtfulness, the project progressed more smoothly for both of us.

So when the stack of projects equals the Empire State Building, or is at least up to your ears, remember that you will somehow get through the day. Breathe. Do the work one step at a time. Get help if necessary, and don't worry if it isn't perfect. If you're a natural perfectionist, ask yourself first if you have time to fine-tooth-comb all the details. If you don't, advises Gladys, make an appointment

with your therapist after work to deal with your frustration, and
do your best. Sometimes it's important to *just do it*, and work out
the details later.

And, last but not least, when all else fails, remember the reality
of the situation: "If everything doesn't get finished in time, probably no one is going to *die*."

COMMUNITY IN THE WORKPLACE

W | e recently held a Temps from Hell meeting to discuss the pros
and cons of temping. The meeting was presided over by
Gladys A. Frumpworth IV, who ordered Chinese take-out to
munch on while we talked. Actually, she ordered enough for ten
voracious temps, although there were only two of us, but Gladys
believes in plenty of food for thought. After declaring the meeting
officially in session, we alternated between eating fried rice with
chopsticks, and writing our ideas on a blackboard with a piece of
red chalk.

Temping pros included:

❖ Variety
❖ Flexibility
❖ Meeting new people
❖ Exposure to different companies

Temping cons (what we call challenges) were:

❖ Transitions
❖ First days
❖ Lack of paid benefits
❖ Absence of community in the workplace

We agreed that our list items were obvious, but viewed absence
of community as an issue in need of clarification. I elaborated:
"This morning I saw a blue heron on my way to work. It was

flying. It was beautiful. I felt real awe. I miss the fact that when I got to work I really had no one to share that feeling with."

Gladys nodded as she dipped an eggroll into spicy mustard. Her green eyes watered, and she chewed thoughtfully. She reminded me of the other side, of veteran temps who argue that a benefit of temping is the *lack* of community involved. My friend Tina is one of those temps. "You get so tired of office politics," Tina says. "It's much easier to do the job and go home with no attachment. As a temp, you don't have to worry about that stuff. No fuss, no muss."

I can't deny the truth of this. Office politics can do a great deal of personal damage to companies and their employees. But, unless we have hermit tendencies, community is generally something that human beings need to seek out on some level for the sake of our emotional and physical health. Sociological studies show that people who have the support of a community tend to be sick less often, and illnesses heal more quickly in people who have community connections. It's natural to expect these connections from a job situation, since we spend so many hours at work.

As it takes time to mesh with any social group, community is difficult to come by for the temporary worker. For one thing, there is frequently too little time to establish rapport. (Gladys compares this to a vegetable soup that is better on the second or third day, "after the ingredients have gotten acquainted.") For another thing, because temps function outside of the traditional employment structure, they are cut off from familiar sources of belonging. While people may generally agree that a person should be accepted whether he or she is a president, janitor, or temp, this practice isn't always naturally followed. Temps aren't *automatically* welcomed into a company community; they have to prove themselves first. Therefore, isolation is a common feeling among people in the temporary work force.

Even after years of temping, I still sometimes encounter isolation as I feel myself operating outside the social circle of companies, and as I search for someone to share my blue heron with. Fortunately, I have an internal support system—Gladys—who sympathizes. She urges me to get past my isolation feelings and:

❖ *Make it a point to reach out to people in a work situation.* Often, permanent employees don't understand that a temp *wants* community, so they don't make the first move. They may think that the temp is a loner by nature.

❖ *Try to find at least one person to relate to on a personal level at work.* One or two satisfying conversations during the day can create the difference between feeling like an outsider and feeling connected.

❖ *Enhance community situations outside of the workplace.* Family, friends, social organizations, and community work can provide important interaction.

❖ *Remember that any group situation is a potential community.* Communities come in many forms. If you use public transportation, regular passengers can be daily connections. Impromptu conversations while standing in line at the grocery store, perusing the new fiction section at the library, or sharing a long elevator ride all can have a sense of connecting with others.

❖ *Offer spontaneous community in any situation.* Gladys tries to interact with people when she is out walking. Recently she stopped to chat with a temporary laborer who was putting up a fence near a road construction site. As she continued on her walk, she realized that she had provided some form of community in that man's workplace.

❖ *Get involved in some kind of activity—spiritual, creative, or otherwise—that gives you a sense of well-being.* One temp I know takes yoga classes. Another does modern dance. Some are active in their church. Belonging to a Zen meditation center has contributed greatly to my success in the realm of temporary work. The group offers a strong social circle. Meditation reminds me to slow down, to experience each moment as it occurs, and to count on myself—to not be so caught up in what others are doing or thinking. Which makes it easier for me to realize how many opportunities for community exist on every assignment, and to have fewer expectations of others.

On the subject of expectations, one such concern in doing temporary work involves holidays. While most holidays pass by uneventfully, Christmas can be a challenge because it's the time of year when the community spirit of a company most shows itself. Of course, people may try to pull you in, or go out of their way to include you in the festivities, and there can be a sense of celebration. On the other hand, Christmas is the time of year when feelings of being an outsider are most likely to arise for a temporary worker.

I have experienced both sides of the coin. One year I had a hand in arranging a company Christmas party that turned out to be quite enjoyable. The following season, at another business, I was asked to acquire information and make reservations at a restaurant for an office Christmas bash that I wasn't even invited to. Admittedly, it was an occasion of hurt feelings for this seasoned Temp from Hell. Gladys kindly pointed out that I had often wondered if the people in question were human beings or robots, and now I knew the answer! When we finished laughing over that, she also noted that this was a rare incident, unlikely to be encountered twice. We agreed that the best way to handle future holidays was by having fewer expectations. And by sending telepathic empathy to the unsuspecting temps who got stuck with the robots in subsequent years.

Having discussed all of this, Gladys and I finished our chow mein and reached for the fortune cookies. Oddly enough, we received the same fortune: "You will be successful in any gathering."

Hoping that this would be true, we adjourned the meeting of the Temps from Hell. I got ready for my next assignment, and Gladys took the rest of the food to the homeless shelter down the street.

NEGOTIATING

A friend once commented that I usually manage to come up with assignments that offer a large degree of flexibility—flex-time, decreased hours, days off, increased responsibilities and increased wages—whereas she gets stuck with the standard temporary eight-to-fives. How do I do it? she wants to know. She's tried negotiating many times, she says, but it doesn't work. What do I do that she doesn't?

The truth is that my assignments aren't radically different from hers. I've had my share of those eight-to-fives, ones that involve a rigid noon-to-one lunch hour and are heavily punctuated with rules and regulations. The only difference between my friend and me is that *I* have an in-house tutor, Gladys A. Frumpworth IV, who taught me how to create the flexibility myself—by negotiating.

The first step is to determine if the situation is appropriate to your planned negotiation. An assignment that involves heavy telephones or production work, for instance, offers less leeway due to scheduling details; someone has to be there to cover those areas. Negotiating may also be less of an option at a conservative company that has more established policies and procedures. And negotiating may not be worth the effort if the job is short-term, a week or less. Most of the time, however, negotiations are possible, if they are handled with consideration for the clients involved.

Negotiating on a temporary assignment depends on a combination of attitude, timing, and direct communication. There are two basic techniques. The first is straightforward. You simply arrive at the job site, meet the people, and plunge into the workload. At some point during the morning you mention casually that you need to leave at a certain time—say, 4:30 instead of 5:00. You also mention that you hope this isn't an inconvenience. Usually this is no problem and the client is willing to go along with it. Of course, if the time adjustment *is* inconvenient for the employer, you understand, and remain with the established hours.

The second negotiating technique is more delicate, and involves a progression of steps:

1. *Work within the given boundaries of the job in the beginning.* Concentrate on putting your best foot forward and doing the work well. At the same time, mentally assess the situation to determine if the company is open to your preferred changes.

2. *Establish rapport.* Get to know the people and initiate relationships. This may take some time, depending on the business and the people. Show the client that you have a good attitude and are reliable. From here you can decide if the situation is open to negotiating.

3. *Speak directly to your supervisor.* If he or she is particularly busy, leave a note or electronic mail message that can be answered at a convenient time. If you are working through an agency, don't worry about updating them on small details. They don't want to know that you have a dentist appointment on Wednesday, or that you want to take a half hour instead of a full hour for lunch. They do want you to communicate effectively with the client.

4. *Don't negotiate just to negotiate.* One of the advantages of temporary work is the option to initiate flexibility. On occasion, temps take advantage of their temporary role as a way to assert power over employers. I've discovered that it works better to be sensitive to the situation, to negotiate only when it is agreeable to everyone. Otherwise, it's easy to slide into a role of "crying wolf," which ultimately backfires.

5. *Make a reasonable request that is feasible for the employer.* A shorter lunch hour and small adjustments in arrival or departure time are fair requests to begin with. Days off, tasks you would prefer not to do, increased responsibilities and wages, and the like, might be better worked up to.

6. *Wait until the moment is right.* It's not worth your while to negotiate with someone who doesn't like to carry on a conversation before his morning cup of coffee, or who has a deadline to meet.

7. *Be self-confident.* A professional, pleasant tone of voice, eye

contact, and solid stance are convincing. Know exactly what you want to say.

8. *Words should be brief and to the point.* Try phrases such as, "Would it be possible for me to take half an hour instead of an hour at lunch?" or "I need to have Wednesday off for personal business. I hope this isn't a problem for you." If the situation seems to call for it, offer a specific reason, e.g., "I have a class at four-thirty," or "I have a job interview."

9. *When a negotiation is successful, make it worth the client's while.* Continue to have a positive attitude, and continue to do a good job. Don't relax and figure that it's all downhill from here. Perhaps even do a *better* job to show that you appreciate the company's willingness to be flexible to your needs.

10. *If a negotiation* isn't *successful, accept it.* Negotiating is give and take. You win some, you lose some. But if you feel strongly about a certain issue, don't back down. Gladys once went to a word-processing assignment that involved covering an hour a day on a busy switchboard. Knowing that telephone work is not among her skills and, therefore, not to the benefit of the client, she apologetically declined. When the client pursued this issue, Gladys explained by saying that she would not have accepted the assignment had the agency mentioned telephones. She offered to be replaced by another temp or to take on an alternate responsibility. The client thanked her for her honesty and kept her on.

Be aware that winning a negotiation can create an awkward work environment by setting you apart from permanent employees. They may resent what they view as you acquiring special privileges over them. A sticky situation, indeed. So sticky, in fact, that Gladys and I devoted an entire Temps from Hell meeting to the subject. We held the meeting over tea and crumpets, to remind ourselves of the importance of politeness at all times. As Gladys said, "There is something screamingly civilized about tea and crumpets." While sipping our tea, holding our cups just so, and wiping the crumbs daintily from our lips, we arrived at the following list.

❖ Don't talk about a successful negotiation, even if it was hard-won. Don't mention it at all unless necessary, because it may create a departmental rift. If permanent employees aren't permitted to adjust their hours or take time off, there will likely be resentment toward temps who ask to bend the rules.

❖ If you must mention your negotiation, and you sense resistance, apologize for any inconvenience that it might cause other employees. Offer to accommodate them in other ways, as by taking a later lunch hour or helping with a large project.

❖ Maintain a professional, pleasant attitude. Let people know that you are still willing to work with them. It's difficult to resent a person who is doing the work and is sincerely kind.

Of course, Gladys and I agreed that it isn't necessary to negotiate on *every* job. Some assignments do come with hours and wages that are satisfactory. But the option usually exists. After all, the main advantage of temporary work is flexibility, of which the temp is the creator. We adjourned the meeting on this note, after negotiating to share the last crumpet.

WHEN THERE'S NOTHING TO DO

T here will be more work, the boss assures you, but she doesn't know when. Grimly, she implies: Please Look Busy. Other employees and clients disapprove when they see someone doing nothing (especially when *they* have enough work to blast them into the next century).

Look Busy. Also known as "There's Nothing to Do, but Look Like There's Plenty of Work to Do." And while you're at it, Look Like You're Swamped. This means no items that make it obvious that you're goofing off:

❖ No Gothic novels
❖ No newspapers

❖ No jigsaw puzzles
❖ No solitaire
❖ And no (no! no!) computer games (especially ones that make noise)

It means no personal phone calls and no personal grooming. Filing is okay, but not the kind that involves fingernails.

Look Busy. This also translates as:

❖ Don't talk to people who are trying to work.
❖ Don't attempt to break the Guinness Record of the longest chain of paper clips.
❖ Don't hold a Temps from Hell meeting (or any non-work-related meeting) in the middle of the office.
❖ Don't break out your lunch two hours early.
❖ Don't sneak out before it's time to go home.
❖ And, whatever you do, don't sit quietly and stare into space!

On the other hand, it's okay to read this book, check the clock, straighten your desk, check the clock, organize the already organized supply closet, check the clock again, water the plants that were just watered, check the clock, go to the bathroom several times, check the clock, sharpen pencils, check the clock, dust the top of your computer, and do a number of other things that are equally as boring and unproductive. The problem with this is that when you next check the clock (for the hundredth time), you realize that a scant three minutes have passed. At this rate, it takes a light-year to get through one day!

So what do you do?

As a novice temp, I couldn't believe that this was happening to me, so I called the temporary agency to complain. They couldn't believe I was calling.

"Learn new software," they suggested. "Teach yourself Lotus 1-2-3. Learn Draw Perfect. Unlock the mysteries of Harvard Graphics. You'll be more marketable!"

More marketable? I grumbled to myself as I turned on the computer. It was sparsely furnished. Not one software program that I didn't already know. I went to the bathroom again, supplied the plants with another cup of water, resharpened the pencils *and* the erasers, checked the clock, and called the agency back.

"What's your problem?" they growled impatiently.

"Surely there must be *something* to do," I repeated.

"Don't worry about it," they sniffed. "We wish *we* were getting paid to do nothing."

A fact of temporary work is that you're sometimes "on retainer"—being paid to be there in the event that a project comes up. In essence, being paid to do nothing. While it may sound crazy, for many employers this is actually preferable to spending precious minutes explaining procedures to someone who is only going to be around for a short duration. Why bother to have a temp? you might ask. Wouldn't the company be saving money if they let you go home? Certainly. But the truth is that they want you there *just in case*. They want that work space occupied. And, for the sake of other employees and visiting clients, they want the person in that work space to look busy.

Of course, it's possible that someone other than your immediate supervisor might need help. Ask around. Someone may appreciate it. If the answer is no, however, let it be known that you are available if they change their minds, and leave it at that; broken records are not appreciated. Then be creative about finding something else to pass the time. Here are several hints that Gladys A. Frumpworth IV passed along:

❖ Write letters on computer or notepad.
❖ Write *anything*. Grocery lists, things-to-do-after-work lists, holiday gift lists, what-you-want-to-do-when-you-grow-up lists. Write in your journal. The mere fact of writing makes you look busy.
❖ Figure out your budget. The mere fact of using a calculator makes you look busy.
❖ Read software manuals (unless they make you sleepy).
❖ Design your own business cards or stationery with desktop publishing programs.
❖ Read books from the office bookshelves. This is a good plan, particularly if you're temping for a book publisher. If not, any

business-oriented books will do. Learn about negotiation techniques, general business practices, sales strategies, etc. In a
pinch, telephone books and reference books will do. It's amazing how exciting the dictionary suddenly becomes when it's the
last resort.

❖ Pay attention to the office plants. Prune. Fertilize. Wash their
leaves. They will enjoy it, it's good for the environment, and you
can take cuttings to root at home later.

❖ Pretend you're on hold on the telephone. This gives you the license to do nothing while "holding."

❖ Read the employee handbook. Sometimes rules and regulations
can be very entertaining.

❖ Clean out the files, both on computer and in the file cabinets.
Gladys has come across interesting résumés and even love letters, which she equates to watching soap operas at work.

❖ Listen to your personal stereo. Do this while pretending to work
on the computer or clean out files. Listen to music, books on
cassette, self-help or meditation tapes. Learn Polish or Swahili.
Listen to a tape of your sweetie singing "Oh, Susanna" in the
shower. Listen to a tape of Gladys A. Frumpworth IV giving
hints about what to do when there's nothing to do, in her me-
lodious gravelly voice.

❖ Surreptitiously do crossword puzzles or cryptoquotes. Hide
them behind an enormous reference book so it looks like you're
working on a weighty problem. Push your glasses down on your
nose and act nonchalantly serious. This will make you look
truly intellectual. Co-workers will swoon with admiration.

❖ Take short walks around the office building. Explore unknown
hallways. Snoop in corners. Open doors, unless they say something official like "President" or a term for the opposite sex.

❖ If all else fails, use your imagination. Imagine you and the boss
switching places, even to the point of the clothes you're wearing. Imagine the most conservative people in the office wearing
tiger-striped pajamas. Imagine Martians invading the building.
Imagine what you will be doing twenty years from now. (Hint:
it will probably be something different than what you're doing
now.)

If none of these ideas appeals to you, and you're dying to read your favorite book, go ahead, but find an appropriate jacket to disguise it. *Business Strategies in the '90s* should do nicely. Or typeset your own cover on computer: *How to Be the Perfect Temp.* Another option is to arrange a pile of three-ring binders on your desk so that no one can sneak up on you. Read with one eye on the rest of the room.

Sure, look busy when necessary, but find other alternatives to watching the clock. You'll be an expert in no time. In fact, Gladys has become such an expert that one boss was reluctant to assign a new project because she appeared so focused on her work. What was she really doing? Plotting her biorhythms for the next fifty years!

"BE EXCELLENT TO EACH OTHER"

B eing in contact with so many people during the course of my temporary career has made me aware of the degrees of sincerity (or insincerity) exhibited in daily conversation. It's amazing how often someone asks "How are you?" only to walk away before the other person can respond. Ouch!

No matter how prevalent this pattern is in our society today, it still hurts to be on the receiving end of such an exchange. Without thinking, the person who walks away is telling the other person that he or she isn't important. Which may create a domino effect, as in this conversation with my friend Ian:

> *Me (cheerfully):* Hi! How are you?
> *Ian (grouchily):* Do you care?
> *Me (tentatively):* Of course.
> *Ian (hesitantly):* Are you sure?
> *Me (emphatically):* Yes!
> *Ian (suspiciously):* Really?
> *Me (annoyed):* Would you please tell me what's going on?

It turned out that a few hours earlier, the bookkeeper at his current temporary job had inquired about his weekend. Pleased to be asked, he was prepared to respond. But as he began to recount a concert that he attended on Saturday night, she literally turned her back on him and entered numbers into her calculator. The result was that Ian felt shunned and took it out on the next person he spoke with—me.

As temps, we are more apt to experience inadvertent insincerity in the workplace, simply because people don't know us and we don't know them. Why become acquainted with someone we may never see again? is a common attitude of both permanent workers and temps. Permanent workers may think they don't have time, that their busy schedules are more important than a new face in the office. They may not consider that a temp appreciates being greeted or conversed with. Or they may simply feel that temps have nothing directly to do with them, so there is no point in personal contact.

For the same reasons, temps might be inclined to think that the idea of temping is merely to enter a situation, do the work, and move on to another company. Why put in the effort? But then, why not? This contact with a variety of people is the perfect place for opening up avenues of communication. For asking people about themselves, and hearing what they have to say. For promoting general good will or "excellence" toward others.

This reminds me of a silly movie called, *Bill & Ted's Excellent Adventure*, where the characters say, "Be excellent to each other," as a matter of course. "Good morning, excellent mailman!" they say, and "How are you, excellent secretary?" Be excellent to each other!

Though I don't recall details of most of the film, I immediately adopted the "Be excellent to each other" slogan for my own. In fact, I like it so much that whenever I begin a new job, I make a "Be Excellent" sign and hang it above my work station. Mostly I do this as a personal reminder, to prompt myself to be pleasant, even when faced with crabby people or doing tasks that I don't enjoy. Even when I'm in a bad mood. To remind myself to be excellent by:

❖ Smiling at people
❖ Fully listening to people
❖ Paying complete attention to the person I'm with
❖ Asking if I can be of help in any way

So far, the effect of the sign has been positive on both myself and others. Initially, it helps me to feel excellent about myself, which reminds me to extend that generosity to others. At this point, co-workers often take the cue, as in these two successive jobs, where my message came full circle.

On the first assignment, I went away on a trip for a few days. When I returned, I found a note on my desk: "Welcome back, Excellent Deborah! We missed you!"

On my last day of the second assignment, I received an electronic mail message: "You are excellent! I'm really going to miss your cheerful attitude. Thanks for being an inspiration to me." The domino effect again—but in a positive vein.

Speaking of domino effects, I recently spoke with my friend Ian:

> *Me (cheerfully):* Hi! How was your weekend?
> *Ian (thoughtfully):* Do you have time to hear about it?
> *Me (sincerely):* Sure.
> *Ian (shyly):* You're not going to believe this, but remember the bookkeeper from my last job?
> *Me (interestedly):* Yes.
> *Ian (grinning):* We went to the movies.
> *Me (surprised):* You're kidding! What happened?
> *Ian (cheerfully):* Well, I made a "Be Excellent" sign and hung it over my desk. The next day she came over to say that she liked it. And things progressed from there.

Wow! How much more excellent can you get?

Gladys just reminded me that while we're being excellent to people, we can also express concern for the environment. As temps, we can dust or water office plants if we see that it's needed. We can conserve energy by turning out lights when they're not in use. We can also recycle. Paper can be saved by printing out only documents that are necessary, making double-sided copies, and drinking coffee out of ceramic (not paper) cups. If the assignment is long-term and the company doesn't recycle, we can do them a favor and help set up a recycling program. Gladys has been a fierce recycling temp ever since she discovered that one business she worked for used 136 trees per day in paper—or 49,640 trees per year.

So be excellent to each other. Be excellent to yourself. Be excellent to the environment. Weaving in and out of businesses with our "Be Excellent" message, we may have a greater impact than we think.

DIFFICULT RELATIONSHIPS

T he last chapter was about being excellent to people. But what happens if you find yourself confronted with someone you *can't* be excellent to? Unfortunately, for all of us, this happens more than we'd like.

Being a successful temp sometimes requires assuming the role of amateur psychologist to stay a step ahead of difficult people. Gladys A. Frumpworth IV decided this midway through her temporary career when she bestowed an honorary psych-out degree upon herself. Her reasoning was that, since she would be working with more personalities than most "permanent" employees see in a lifetime, she needed all the help she could get.

In obtaining this self-appointed degree, the most difficult lesson that Gladys faced was not to take difficult people personally—to realize that sometimes people could be in a bad mood or act like jerks for one reason or another—and it didn't necessarily have anything to do with her.

Her second major challenge involved ignoring people's egos, which she discovered to be virtually wall-to-wall in every company she temped at. Gladys elaborates in her notes:

"Egos are nasty beasts with hairy eyeballs, mountain-sized teeth, and barks that are louder than God's. There is always a tendency to fight egos with your own ego, but this is like fighting fire with fire. It never works. Better to take the advice of Zen master Dainin Katagiri-roshi: 'If somebody barks at you, don't bark back!' "

Gladys's third lesson involved not taking herself too seriously on the job. Understanding that staying one step ahead of people, "psyching them out," didn't mean that she was better than anyone, but that she could use her observations to work more effectively with others. A challenging lesson indeed.

After flunking, reflunking, and, finally, *unflunking* these lessons, Gladys felt able to be more objective, to be unconditionally nice to people, and to see the humor in a situation. She also wanted to share her experience with others. Herewith, a handful of "case studies" of challenging supervisors and co-workers, their "diagnoses," and the Frumpworth analysis of how to deal with them.

CASE STUDY NO. 1: THE ROBOT

He sits at his desk all day, mechanically staring at numbers on the computer screen. If someone tells a joke in his presence, he fails to see the humor, although his face is set in a perpetual smile. He is the type of person who asks about your weekend, then walks away before you have a chance to answer. If anyone ever said "Be excellent" to him, it was spoken in a language that he didn't understand.

The best way to handle the Robot is to keep interaction brief, concentrate on your work, remember that you're getting paid, and don't take him too seriously. Realize that the Robot isn't as comfortable with people as he is with numbers. Feelings are foreign to him. If you suddenly develop the raging flu and tell him that you have to leave immediately, don't be surprised if he says, "Can you make these photocopies before you go?" It's okay to shake your head, and run for the door. One good thing about the Robot is that he quickly forgets. You'll be tuned out of his robotic database by the time you've reached your car.

CASE STUDY NO. 2: THE PRESSURE COOKER

No matter what project is on the front burner, the Pressure Cooker considers it life and death. When she issues a new assignment, she panics if someone puts it on the back burner for a few minutes while he finishes his current project. "It's not a big deal" is the worst thing you can say to a Pressure Cooker. It's guaranteed to make her blow her top. Better to make her your priority, at least for the moment. Calmly explain your strategy for completing the project. Be specific about deadlines. Ask for her input.

The Pressure Cooker cools down considerably when she is able to imagine the project completion. Of course, she will check at intervals to make sure that things are in order, but then it's full steam ahead, with less likelihood of anyone being burned.

CASE STUDY NO. 3: THE NIT-PICKER

Any task is impossible for the Nit-Picker until he disposes of the piece of lint that is staring ominously at him from the carpet across the room. Only when it is safely in the trash does he explain your new project. When you request details, he says, "Just do it. Then I'll tell you what's wrong." This is typical for the Nit-Picker. No matter how hard you work, there is always *plenty* wrong.

It helps to remember that there is plenty wrong with everything else in his life, too. He is disappointed with the person who works on his car, the person who paints his house, the person who cuts his hair, the people who are his parents, and the person who is his wife. Furthermore, he can provide a complete list of all the things that are wrong with the world at large. In fact, nothing has ever been good enough for him from the moment he was born. So, if *you* expect to be the first perfect thing in his life, you are definitely in the wrong place.

"Do your best and don't worry about it" is the best advice for dealing with a Nit-Picker. On the positive side, if you can keep your expectations down, and realize that his perfectionism isn't your problem, you'll know that at least he's being sincere when he says something nice. Also, you may be able to see that the Nit-Picker has a kind heart. If your car is in the shop, he insists that you borrow his Mercedes. At Christmas, you can expect a nice card, a bottle of good champagne, *and* an invitation to his Christmas party. And you might even have a good time if you ignore his criticism of the single white cat hair on your black velvet dress as he greets you at the door.

CASE STUDY NO. 4: THE CONTROL FREAK

The Control Freak needs complete control over everything that occurs in her office. She might even eavesdrop on a staff member while he's on the telephone and criticize what is being said as he speaks. This way, *everyone* knows that *she* is in charge.

If this behavior becomes chronic, the staff member has no choice but to confront the Control Freak, since such interruptions are nonproductive. She should first be approached directly in a nonthreatening manner: "Is there a problem with the information I'm giving out?" She may have a valid suggestion. If she says that there is no problem, gently ask her to refrain from commenting while you're on the telephone, since it is difficult to hear the client. The next time she interrupts, say to the client, "Excuse me, my supervisor would like to speak with you," hand the phone to her, and go get a cup of coffee. After a few such incidents, the Control Freak will probably feel validated that she is indeed in charge. Then she will attend to her own work and leave her staff to accomplish theirs—at least for a while.

CASE STUDY NO. 5: THE BIG SHOT

The Big Shot's business is so small that his office is a scant nine square feet, and he has only one part-time temporary secretary. Still, he insists on professionalism. There is a strict dress code and an employee handbook of established policies. He has a plant service, which consists of two scrawny ferns, and a maintenance person, who stops by twice a week to water and fertilize. When he has a single piece of paper to photocopy, he walks *past* the copier to give it to his secretary.

The Big Shot is like a small dog who wants to be an enormous dog, so he barks loudly to compensate for his size. Having an amicable relationship with the Big Shot depends upon treating him with the seriousness and respect that he craves. Give him what he needs. What do you have to lose? It also helps to concentrate on the work at hand, and tune him out on occasion with a radio and headphones.

CASE STUDY NO. 6: THE SUBSTANCE ABUSER

The Substance Abuser is invariably in a bad mood in the morning and seems magically transformed in the afternoon, after she has her "lunch." At this point, she becomes loud, verbally abuses co-workers, slurs her words, and falls over her desk. A sad situation, indeed.

While many substance abusers are inconspicuous and pose no threat to co-workers in the office, this person clearly presents a problem to herself and others. Especially when she behaves this way on a daily basis. As a temporary worker, you really have no recourse except to avoid the individual as much as possible, appeal to a supervisor, or remove yourself completely from the situation.

After presenting her case studies at a Temps from Hell meeting, someone asked Gladys, "Do you ever *tell* people that they're being difficult, that you simply can't be excellent to them? Do you do this as a 'legacy' for other temps?" Gladys responded with a prudent "It depends on the situation." Certainly, this approach wouldn't work with the Substance Abuser or the Nit-Picker. And telling the Robot would only alienate him further. Gladys once had a difficult boss who literally asked for it by inquiring if she had enjoyed the assignment. Without elaborating, she replied calmly that he had been "quite a challenge," which she felt was adequate to convey the message.

Another way to gently inform difficult people is by using humor. Gladys tried this with a man who regularly shouted for his employees from his office, instead of using the intercom or walking to their desks to speak with them. The employee was then supposed to drop whatever he was doing and run in to answer a question or perform some trivial task. No one appreciated this behavior, but no one dared to say anything for fear of being fired. As a temp, Gladys was exempt from termination, so she decided to ignore Katagiri-roshi's advice not to bark back and instead to take matters into her own hand.

One day, after he shouted her name, Gladys remained at her desk and barked. When he didn't hear her, she barked again—with more emphasis this time. At the third bark, he left his office and stared at her, looking perplexed. After a minute, he scratched his head and said, "Are you trying to tell me that I'm treating you like a dog?"

To which Gladys grinned and panted.

While we can't report that there was a 100 percent improvement, she admits that the shouting was thereafter kept to a minimum (reinforced by periodic short barks), and she was able to end the difficult relationship on an excellent note. A note that Gladys always recommends.

JOB RECOGNITION

E verybody deserves a pat on the back. A handshake. A few words of praise. Is this too much to ask? Some people say it is, that employees are rarely recognized for work well done—particularly temps. So how do you get recognition on the job? Consider the following situation.

I labored long and hard on a successful desktop publishing manual, only to overhear my project partner taking full credit for the work. This woman was obviously proud of herself as she recalled details of certain phases and nights when she worked past midnight. She even recounted problems that arose (as I had recounted them to her) and how she resolved them.

She summed it up accurately: "It was a long struggle, but certainly worth it." Her co-workers were visibly impressed.

When we were alone, I immediately reproached her. She seemed surprised at my anger.

"You're so nice that I didn't think you would mind," she said. "Besides," she added, "you're just a temp. Does it really matter so much?"

It was my turn to be surprised. Of course it mattered! And what difference did it make that I was a temp? Yes, even as a temp, the project was important to me. I wanted credit loud and clear. I wanted my name stamped in gold all over the pages. I wanted to climb to the top of my mountain of paperwork and toot my own horn.

Because if I didn't do it, nobody would.

Sometimes, as a temp, it's important to give yourself recognition—to climb to the top of that stack of paper and shout praises for yourself. Pat yourself on the back. Put a feather in your cap. Why? Because if you don't do it, nobody will. Because most managers don't sit around quietly noticing your progress and awarding brownie points. But haven't we been taught that singing our own praises isn't *nice*? And aren't temps just filling in the gaps, only to move on to something else? Not necessarily.

In the above case, receiving credit for my desktop publishing work meant more challenging (and higher-paying) assignments at this company in the future. Assignments that I knew would be available to me if I was recognized for the current project. Assignments that would *not* be available if my partner took all the credit for herself. When I recovered from my anger, I realized that she actually did me a favor by pointing out how I came across. Obviously, that "nice" person had to go. Enter Gladys A. Frumpworth IV, the Temp from Hell.

Gladys immediately assumed a take-charge attitude. She confidently and quietly informed people (not just her partner) of her project status, and casually mentioned how she solved difficult issues. She made it a point to learn as much as she could. At the same time, she managed to resolve the conflict with her partner, to work as a team. She tooted her own horn by doing a good job. As a result, her supervisor got a sense of her accomplishments. Resulting in more challenging projects *and* a raise.

Whether you're a temporary or permanent employee, credit ought to be given where it's due. In seeking recognition, it is sometimes helpful to assess your motivation.

❖ Will recognition better qualify you for more challenging projects in the future, either from the temporary agency, or through the business itself?

❖ Will acknowledgment qualify you for a raise?

❖ If your wish is to go permanent with the company, will credit assist you in meeting that goal?

All of these are valid reasons for expecting recognition. They serve to work toward a professional goal and they contribute to the company involved. On the other hand, it's equally important to recognize when acknowledgment *doesn't* depend on other people, when it is used only for bolstering self-esteem or to impress others, or when it can take the form of self-satisfaction instead. Such self-satisfaction may be gained from a self-taught computer program, the experience of which can be carried to another job. It may stem from brainstorming on a co-worker's project, or offering moral support in any fashion.

Self-satisfaction doesn't even need to come from the job itself. You might gain the sense of a job well done from giving directions to someone on the way to work, or from having listened to a distressed friend on the telephone the night before. Maybe you're pleased with the progress you made in your modern dance class this week, and you can carry that pleasure with you to work. There are many areas in life from which to find personal acknowledgment.

Back on the job, receiving credit for your work is one thing, but what about tedious or repetitive tasks such as making photocopies, taking out the trash, or running office errands? How should a temp handle these assignments?

"With great care," advises Gladys. "Every job should be performed mindfully, whether it's picking up litter or managing a large corporation. Each task has its place."

In the beginning of my temp career I didn't understand her reasoning. After all, I was a writer. Shouldn't I be receiving assignments that were more related to my skills? I asked myself during a week-long filing project. Shouldn't someone else be doing these repetitive tasks? I wondered as I made a thousand photocopies, collated and stapled, for a corporate meeting. And wouldn't it be more appropriate for the boss to ask a waitperson for a cup of coffee? I moaned as my precious ego shattered to hundreds of pieces on the floor.

Instead of sympathizing, Gladys cheerfully swept the pieces into the trash and shook my hand. "Congratulations!" she exclaimed. "You have just gotten rid of a very large burden."

She was prepared to celebrate the occasion with homemade mincemeat pie. She cut a piece for each of us and added a spoonful of whipped cream. "Now you're free to concentrate on the work at hand," she said.

As usual, Gladys was right. When I gave serious thought to these tasks, I soon realized that in doing them (and doing them well), I was affecting many other people. For instance, by shoveling a company's sidewalk I was helping to prevent a possible accident. And by completing a letter without typos I was contributing to an executive's credibility with her client. At the same time, I realized that the millions of people who answered telephones, mopped floors, watered plants, and repaved roads were making life a little easier for others, and helping them to do their jobs. I also recalled that Charlotte Joko Beck, a Zen master in San Diego, supported her family for years by doing secretarial work. And that the writer Peter Matthiessen once worked as a longshoreman. The more I thought about it, the more I saw that creative work, such as writing or design, sometimes caused me to live more inside my head than in the physical situation at hand. I began to see so-called minor tasks as opportunities to keep me in the moment, to keep me connected with the rest of the world.

My friend Valerie experienced this same revelation when she worked at a tree nursery one spring. Her back hurt, it was hot, and she had dirt under her fingernails from transplanting seedlings all day. Bees buzzed around her head, and she was worried about being stung. She kept asking herself how she had gotten from being an accountant to this. But she was working outside, the sky was blue, the sun was shining, and every time she took a breath, the smell of flowers filled her whole being.

"This may sound crazy," she later confided, "but something happened during that job. It suddenly occurred to me that transplanting those seedlings just to transplant them was important. I felt alive in a way that I'd never felt before."

I recently met a security guard at a large corporation who expressed the same outlook. "Some people want to be in charge or have prestigious titles, or be recognized for every small thing they do," she told me, "but I think I have the best job in the whole company. I get to talk to people every day, and I have a wonderful view of the ocean. What could be better than that?"

I was about to agree when Gladys appeared, carrying a box of paper to be recycled. "What could be better indeed!" she echoed as she emptied the box into a large bin. Then she looked at her watch. "Hey, it's five o'clock," she said. "Anyone want to go for a swim?"

SAYING NO

I t is a well-known fact that "No!" was the first word out of the mouth of Gladys A. Frumpworth IV, so she has no problem saying it whenever necessary. But for most of us, saying no requires a little practice. Especially in the workplace. Especially when we're temps. And some of us probably wonder: as temps, do we have the *right*?

"Nonsense!" exclaims Gladys. "Balderdash! *Everyone* has the right to say no."

So there you have it.

"But," she adds, "it's a matter of knowing when."

For which she gives the following guidelines:

❖ Say no when your health is jeopardized (as when you are asked to lift heavy objects or work in a room with toxic fumes).
❖ Say no when your self-respect is compromised (as when you're expected to do projects on your own time).
❖ Say no when your finances are infringed upon (as when you're requested to drive your car for office errands, with no mention of mileage reimbursement).

Granted, some employers don't realize when what they are asking is inappropriate, especially if previous employees have honored the same requests with no complaint.

"Why shouldn't you work straight through the day without taking a break?" they might ask. "My regular word-processor never
takes one."

Or "Why can't you drop these off at the post office after five
o'clock? My other assistants didn't mind."

In the face of such responses, saying no is difficult indeed. In
fact, saying that one small word at any time can be difficult—even
after a hundred temporary assignments. Probably even after a
thousand assignments. Because we're programmed to be nice. To
please our co-workers. To be cheerleaders in the working world.
Clearly, we need to teach ourselves to become better acquainted
with this word, to let it roll freely off our tongues when necessary
to protect ourselves.

I know one temp who practices enunciating "No" in front of a
mirror. Another temp says "No" out loud whenever he thinks
about it. As for myself, I have a talking Gladys doll tucked safely
into my imagination. She has a pull-string in the back of her neck,
just like one of those dolls I used to have as a child. When I mean
to say no, but am tempted to say yes, I reach my hand beneath the
doll's screaming red hair and mentally pull the string. In my mind,
I pull the string ten or twenty times if I need to. After Gladys re-
sponds with a machine-gun-like "No! No! No! No! No! No! No!
No! No! No!" I get the message. I am given courage. Such situations include:

❖ *Moving heavy furniture or equipment.* Particularly if you don't
  have health insurance, or if you are five feet tall and weigh
  ninety-five pounds. Gladys, who is in this category, was once
  astounded by a request to help carry a wooden desk down a
  flight of stairs. "You've got to be kidding!" was her initial response, even though it was a *short* flight. But understanding that
  there was a problem to be solved, she went to find the janitor
  down the hall. He was six feet tall, weighed in at three hundred
  pounds, and could lift that desk with a single hand.
❖ *Moving complicated computer equipment.* This is fragile stuff.
  An expert should do it.
❖ *Performing duties that are radically different from the original*

job description (unless it has been discussed beforehand). "No, sir, I don't do windows!" Gladys says pleasantly when she discovers that a word-processing assignment has been somewhat altered. "And, *no*, I don't write advertising copy either. Unless, of course, you want to pay me extra to do these things."

❖ *Driving your own car for office errands.* This is negotiable, of course, but a mileage reimbursement plan should be worked out in advance. I knew one temp who drove his car an average of thirty miles a week for a company over a four-month period. He didn't ask for compensation, nor did his supervisor offer it. I calculated that, at twenty cents per mile, the business owed him over a hundred dollars.

❖ *Doing office errands after work.* Unless it's possible to leave early enough to finish before your scheduled go-home time, errands should be part of the regular workday.

❖ *A schedule where no breaks are provided.* Even if the "regular" person usually skips breaks. Most state laws require employees to be given a paid break of ten to fifteen minutes every two hours. Computer operators should get away from their terminal screens every hour.

❖ *Projects handed to you before your scheduled work time.* If you arrive at a job fifteen minutes early, this is still your personal time. You don't have to begin a project, unless you're being paid for that extra fifteen minutes.

❖ *Employers who interrupt your lunch hour.* If you eat lunch at your desk, you are especially susceptible to this. But what can you do if the company has no lunchroom and there is no place nearby to go? Try informing co-workers that you are "going to lunch." Or hang a humorous sign over the desk: "Out to Lunch. Will be back at 1 o'clock. Pretend that I am invisible." If someone approaches you with work and uses the excuse that she might forget to talk to you about it later, offer to write a reminder note.

❖ *Overtime.* Unless it's been previously scheduled, an overtime rate has been discussed, and you want to make extra money. Also, if you're working through an agency, most of them require advance permission for overtime.

The above items are offered only as basic suggestions. You may not take issue with using your car for company errands or with working overtime. You may have your own list for saying no. Tina, who hates the smell of coffee, takes offense at being asked to make it. Valerie, who is Jewish, doesn't feel comfortable sending company Christmas cards. These are personal nos and vary with the individual.

Yes, some situations require a firm, polite no, so that employers don't take unnecessary advantage. Being a temp involves paying this basic respect to yourself. Employers pay attention when you set boundaries. Most of them not only listen, but they respect you for it as well.

WHEN A CO-WORKER IS JEALOUS

T here is a green face in the crowd at work—jealousy—and you, the temp, are the target. Why? Because you're a party-crasher, of course, and—how could you?—*you're doing everything perfectly!* This is just for openers. Besides that, you have flexibility, you are given the easy tasks, you have a sense of humor, you dress smartly, you are self-confident, you aren't caught up in the company politics, the boss likes you and says so, you've been places, and, worst of all, *you might have designs on somebody's job.* Oof! No wonder this person is green with envy.

I've encountered jealousy in more than one workplace. In fact, it seems to be a common occurrence in offices in general. When I mentioned this to Gladys, she didn't seem surprised.

"Companies are hotbeds of competition," she told me. "Employees often feel neglected. They don't think that they're appreciated enough for the work they do. When a temp arrives on the scene and is given attention, it may raise deep insecurity issues in permanent employees. This doesn't have anything to do with the temp—not really. It is simply safer to vent insecurities on a temp than on co-workers or on a supervisor." Then she pointed out some of the signs:

❖ Green Face informs you of how much work she does, how much work she took home last night, and how indispensable she is to the company, while receiving little credit. She then lets you know that you are praised because you are given tasks that anyone could easily accomplish.

❖ Green Face catches you making a mistake. She brings it up publicly the first chance she gets.

❖ Green Face gossips about everyone, particularly about the boss who praises you so much. She can supply details of why he isn't a nice person and why you shouldn't like him.

❖ You are warned by Green Face not to use the double-sided feature on the photocopier because it isn't reliable. You appreciate her "friendly" advice and proceed to duplex manually. When someone else enters the room and wonders what you are doing, Green Face becomes your savior: "The duplexer works fine for *me*. Here, let me help you."

"Generally, the green face in any office isn't a mean person. She just wants to be acknowledged. She wants her working environment to be safe," says Gladys.

She emphasizes that, as a temp, your job will be easier if you let her know that you aren't a threat, that you are there to work with her, not against her.

1. Be on the jealous person's side. When she says that she works hard, agree with her. When she tells you how busy she is, offer to help.

2. Offer sincere compliments. If you like her dress, tell her. If you like the way she is doing something, let her know. Whenever possible, compliment her in front of others.

3. If she catches you making a mistake, admit it. Ask her advice about how to do things differently.

4. Imagine yourself in her place. Everyone has been jealous of someone at some time. Try to remember a situation when you were jealous, what the circumstances were, and how painful it

felt. Gladys recalls one of her own green face incidents, when a co-worker received a creative project that she wanted. It was really difficult to be happy for the other person, she admits; she just wanted to crawl under a desk and lick her wounds.

At this point, Green Face usually relaxes within a day or two and accepts you as a potential ally rather than an enemy. Who wouldn't rather have a friend in the office? Unfortunately, sometimes the source of the problem isn't Green Face herself, but other people in the workplace, as with these challenging situations:

Carol temped for Sue at J Company during her two-week vacation. Everyone said that Carol did a wonderful job. In fact, when Sue returned, her co-workers cruelly teased her that Carol's work was superior—yes, they actually said this! Not only that, but these people liked Carol so much that she was invited to sit in during another person's vacation. At a desk adjacent to Sue's.

Not surprisingly, Sue avoided Carol. When Carol discovered why, she could hardly blame her. After Sue rejected several of her efforts to communicate, Carol decided that she had no choice but to let Sue be—the only approach to take if all else fails.

Tom took a temporary position as an electronics technician at Company D, with the hope of going permanent. Tom's supervisor was pleased with his work and regularly praised him in front of James, a permanent employee who had been with the company for a year. Tom noticed that the supervisor never said a positive word to James, although James was a good employee. Sensing probable conflict, Tom made a point of being friendly to James. James didn't seem to trust Tom, however, and ignored him.

After a few months, a job opened up that was a potential promotion for either Tom or James. Now James became openly hostile toward Tom. As Tom pointed out, he couldn't exactly assure James that he wasn't a threat when they were in obvious competition. Tom continued to be as pleasant as possible to James, and to do his best work, while hoping for the job. As it turned out, Tom did get the job. At this point, James stopped speaking to Tom entirely. While Tom understood James's disappointment, he realized with regret that he now had to concentrate on himself. It was difficult for him to accept that there wasn't anything else for him to do.

Most of the time, jealousy in the workplace can be counteracted, but it isn't always possible. Especially when you're up against insensitive supervisors and co-workers. Unfortunately, people don't always realize when they contribute to this problem. As temps, we can do our best to help, but sometimes we just have to do our work and hope that Green Face can take care of herself.

NO TWO JOBS ARE EXACTLY ALIKE

S ometimes temping can be like trying to watch television over the telephone. Let me explain.

I don't have a television, so I once watched *The Wizard of Oz* over the phone. At the time, I was talking to my friend Merlin (who has been a good friend since we met at a temp job several years ago), and he had the movie on his TV set.

Feeling confident because I had seen it more than thirty times, I began to describe the scenes as I listened. At first Merlin was impressed but, as I continued, he pointed out that my descriptions were less than accurate. For instance, I didn't recall at exactly what point Dorothy first encountered the Wicked Witch, or what she said when she liberated the Scarecrow from his post—although I could have sworn that I was right. And I was dead certain that I remembered where the Yellow Brick Road began, but it turned out that I was completely wrong. I knew, of course, that Dorothy's mission was to go home, and that dreams came true on the other side of the rainbow, but other details escaped me.

It was clear that I couldn't really watch television over the telephone.

Temping can be like this. It's easy to become complacent, to think that because you've had thirty or forty temp jobs—or fifty, or one hundred—you already know all the details. Surely, things can't be much different from the last job, you think. Or the one before that. In fact, this assignment is so identical to the one you had a few weeks ago that you could probably do it in your sleep, ho-hum. So you don't pay attention, and instead, your head is full of conversations:

"I will learn this stuff, and then I will go on to something else. No one will know the difference, so why bother?"

"My supervisor looks a lot like my boss at R Company. They even have the same laugh. I bet this guy is a creep, too."

"Why interact with these people when I'm only going to be here for a week?"

Now that you have these things established, and you already know that the job details are boring, you decide to go on a little vacation. Yes, a vacation would do you good. It doesn't matter where to. Anywhere is more interesting than where you are now. So suddenly you're back home in bed, having marvelous dreams. Next you take a side trip to Oz. You're soaring to Paris, flirting in cafés. Ah . . .

The problem with these vacations is that, once they've begun, they are difficult to stop. They are like trying to eat just one tea cookie. They are like stopping after one passionate kiss. I know because I've been there. I've pretended that temp jobs were cafés not only in Paris, but all over the world—which is a lot of cafés. And I've invariably returned to the unhappy news that I typed the wrong page, or spilled a full cup of coffee on an original document, or made fifty copies of the blank side of the paper (the last photocopier I used required the print side to be down, not up). Not only is Gladys giving me the evil eye, but I have to do everything all over again.

Sometimes it's so difficult to remember that no two jobs are exactly alike. Anyway, why bother? Because:

❖ It's more fair to the company and to yourself to be present in your work. Who wants to do things over? It's embarrassing and a waste of time. Also, if you aren't present, you may miss that nice UPS delivery man, whose smile always makes your day, or the plate of homemade fudge that Gladys just set down next to the coffee machine.

❖ You may learn one thing that none of your previous hundred assignments taught you. It doesn't matter if that one thing isn't work-related. My friend Bruce always wanted to learn to play chess and mentioned this to a co-worker on a temp job. The next day the co-worker brought in his chessboard and taught Bruce some strategies over lunch.

❖ The equipment may be just a little different this time. Like the photocopier that copied print-side up instead of print-side down.

❖ Maybe the situation will turn out to be more entertaining than the place you visit in your head. I once went off to a retreat in California, while Valerie moaned the fact that she was stuck at a boring temp job. When we later compared notes, it turned out that my retreat was nothing special, while Valerie's supervisor had managed to set her long blond hair on fire with a lighter— definitely not a boring experience.

❖ People are always interesting. Even the ones who initially seem boring or stupid. Even the ones who are a pain in the neck. You may come across some interesting idiosyncrasies. The boss you think is exactly like the last one may turn out to be the complete opposite. He may be a great guy. He may give you projects that you really enjoy. Or a co-worker that you seem to have nothing in common with may eventually become one of your best friends. You never know.

Someone on a job once saw me drawing multicolored swoosh stripes across some memorandums and said, "Nothing is mundane for you, is it?"

While this isn't necessarily true (as evidenced by all those cafés), I will admit that sometimes the very details that I initially want to avoid are what makes a job the most appealing. Like highlighting memorandums with rainbows instead of plain yellow highlighter. Or using a new typeface on an otherwise unexciting letter. Or putting a little humor into a routine e-mail message.

Get involved with the details and a standard assignment has the potential of being a live film with a compelling plot. With you (or Gladys A. Frumpworth IV) as the star. Like Dorothy in the movie, you always have the option of leaving. But look at the unexpected adventures that she had before she finally got home.

ROMANCE ON THE JOB

Imagine the following situations.

1. It is the first day of a temp job and there she is, the beauty of your wildest dreams, sitting at the next work station. You can't believe your good fortune, especially when she smiles. Not only that, but her eyes are the bluest blue and she has the longest eyelashes. You think you're in love. Could it be that she notices you, too? You can't wait to ask her out. Purrrrrr!

2. You are assigned to act as executive assistant for the president of X Company until he finds a replacement. After a few days, he confides in you about his personal life, including the details of his failing marriage. You catch him staring at you as you type. He tells you that you are wonderful. Then he puts his hand on your shoulder and suggests a drink after work to show his appreciation for everything you've done. You know that he needs someone to talk to; you are a good listener. Maybe his marriage really is failing. You are tempted. Purrrrrr!

3. You are on a long-term technical assignment at a large corporation. You keep meeting a woman from another department on the stairs. There is obvious electricity as you pass by. Chats in passing turn into lunch, then long talks after work. You have everything in common. After several weeks, you suspect this is the person you were meant to spend the rest of your life with. Purrrrrr!

Oh, the ecstasy and agony of falling in love! And at the office, no less. Yes, there is no doubt that an interoffice romance can create a delicate situation. Do you? Or don't you? Or do you—*in time*? It's so hard to decide.

Romance on the job is always an emotional tumble, particularly when you're a temp, and your love interest works in the same department, or is your boss. Will it affect job performance or advancement? Can you successfully juggle romance and a profession in the same environment? Can you make the emotional separation? More difficult decisions.

Out of the corner of my eye, I see Gladys standing over my shoulder, reading this and blushing. She understands the above situations (and more) because, being as red-blooded as anyone, Gladys has had her own on-the-job temptations, including the president who told her more than she wanted to hear about his failing marriage. "Ecstasy and agony, indeed!" she mumbles, shaking her head and admitting that she *almost* fell for being told that she was wonderful, *almost* went for that drink, *almost* made the error of thinking that all the president wanted was talk.

Fortunately, Gladys managed to keep a courteous distance by forcing herself to imagine the inevitable disaster of an off-site "talk" with this man. From that point, she maintained a professional attitude until a replacement was found. But it was enough of a close call to now ask herself the following questions before forging ahead.

❖ What will happen if you romance the company president and his failing marriage suddenly succeeds?

❖ How will you handle it if either of you ends the relationship, and you still have to work directly with the person?

❖ If someone shows interest and it isn't mutual, can you gently offer discouragement, continue to be pleasant, and maintain a professional relationship?

❖ How will you feel if you ask someone out and are rejected? Will sitting at the next work station be uncomfortable?

❖ Does romance at work happen often for you? Will you get a bad reputation (instead of a professional image) with the company or the temporary agency?

❖ Will you be so preoccupied with a romance that you will be unable to concentrate on your work or conduct yourself in a professional manner?

❖ Is the job important to your career?
❖ Is the assignment short enough that a romance won't seriously affect the job?
❖ Is it possible to begin a relationship *after* the assignment is over?
❖ Is it better to have a relationship with someone in a different department, because of the built-in distance?
❖ Is this person *really* the love of your life? Has enough time passed for you to really know?

Of course, advises Gladys, it's probably a good idea to ask yourself these questions at the *beginning* of a job, not in retrospect. It was too late for my friend Lucy, whose life was quickly complicated over a temporary drafting assignment at an architectural firm. The position was in a field that she wanted to break into, and had the possibility of going permanent—or so she thought until she fell in love with one of the architects, who happened to be her boss. They got together for a drink. Dinner followed. Then coffee at her house. And all-night conversations. Purrrrrr!

"It was wonderful, but something wasn't quite right," Lucy later confessed.

It turned out that what wasn't quite right was the architect's estranged girlfriend, who soon reappeared on the scene. Oh, ecstasy followed by agony! Lucy couldn't keep her eyes on her drawing as she watched the architect's girlfriend drop by for lunch. She couldn't stop thinking about how things might have been. Soon her hours were cut to part-time, then to part-part-time. Eventually the work completely dissolved, and she had to scramble for another job.

"It was hard getting rejected by both a man and a job at the same time," Lucy told me when it was over. "I didn't feel like getting out of bed in the morning. But I had to pay the rent. I had to eat, so I had to find another assignment. Oh, if only I had waited before getting involved!"

Of course, every situation is different, and your office romance may be nothing like Lucy's. You may be one of the lucky ones. I know temps who have found future spouses in the next department of a large corporation, and temps who have enjoyed long-term romances with people they met on three-day jobs. My cousin Mark met his wife, Wendy, at a temporary job waiting tables at the Marriott in San Francisco. Now Mark works as a draftsman, Wendy is an accountant, and they are the parents of a baby boy. Yes, true romance *can* occur on the job. If you suspect, however, that romance might jeopardize an important professional connection, or that it will be more agony than ecstasy, it might be better to take a cue from Gladys, who romances men she meets *away* from work, or purrs safely at home—with her cat.

STRESS!

woke up one Sunday morning, only to realize that it was actually Monday, I had overslept, there was nothing in the house for breakfast, and Gladys A. Frumpworth IV had left for work without me. When I got to the office, I already had enough projects to fill a deluxe-sized dump truck, my supervisor was in the process of generating more work, and my computer had gone on strike. To make matters worse, Gladys was perched on top of my desk, looking absolutely radiant.

"What's wrong?" she wanted to know when she saw my frown.

"It's barbaric to have to be anywhere at eight in the morning," I growled.

"Does this mean you're in a bad mood?"

I glowered.

"That's okay," she chirped. "Everyone is in a bad mood sometimes. Even the Temp from Hell." She smiled sympathetically. "Here, read this."

She handed me a sheet of paper. At the top, in bold type, it said:

Are you a temp? Do you suffer from stress? Do you feel that because you're a temp, it isn't acceptable to be in a bad mood or have a hard day at work?

"I can't stand it," I groaned. "Why do you bother to type this stuff up?"

"Because sometimes things make more sense when they're written down," she explained. "Also, you can reread it whenever you need to."

I groaned again and cursed the fact that I had an alter ego who was amiable, practical, *and* a morning person. "Why don't you do something useful, like fix this computer?"

Gladys smiled. "You'll survive," she assured me, and disappeared to find a manual typewriter.

Despite myself, I continued to read:

Did you get up on the wrong side of the bed?

Do you have too much work, a deadline, and a machine that has just broken down at the time when you need it most?

Did someone hurt your feelings?

Do you feel that you can't communicate with the people around you?

Are you just plain in a bad mood?

Do you feel like being by yourself?

You aren't alone! Everyone experiences stress on the job, whether they are a permanent or temporary employee. The thing to remember is not to repress your feelings, but to figure out a way to work with them—now. An informal survey of temps lists how they handle stress on the job.

1. If someone asks you how you are and you're having a bad day, admit it, and say that it will probably go away soon. That way, no one thinks that it's his or her fault.

2. Go for a short walk around the building, or outside.

3. Take a short tea break.

4. Eat a healthy snack (preferably something crunchy like what a rabbit or a bird would enjoy).

5. Read an escapist novel for a few minutes. (Not one that you absolutely can't put down.)*

6. Listen to soothing music on your personal stereo.

7. Make a lunch date with a friend.

8. Take lunch early.

9. Go to the library or a bookstore at noon and read books on relaxation techniques.
10. Have a short cry in the bathroom.
11. Sign up for lunch-hour aerobics.
12. Take a few minutes to work a crossword puzzle.*
13. If you live nearby, go home at lunch or break time and pet your cat or play with your dog. (A little unconditional love goes a long way.)
14. Make an after-work appointment to get a massage.
15. Remind yourself that stress is a passing phase, that you will be feeling better in time. (If it isn't a passing phase, maybe it's caused by something that you need to take care of outside of the assignment. Or maybe it's time to stop doing temporary work altogether, and find one supportive job.)

* Note: it's important to do stress-relieving activities such as crossword puzzles and reading away from your desk so that people won't think you're goofing off.

When I finished reading the list, I had to admit that, as usual, Gladys had a point. After all, she spoke from the experience of a temp who once fought off stress by booking a company conference room all to herself. Leaving a note on her work station that said, "In orbit—be back in 30 minutes," she entered the conference room, locked the door, lay down on the carpet, and took a short nap. (She asked another temp to check on her, in case she didn't wake up in time.) When she returned to her desk, stress had apparently gotten bored with hanging around; it was nowhere to be seen.

There are many ways to give yourself a break from stress on the job. When Gladys isn't napping in conference rooms, she takes an afternoon off or practices meditation techniques. Valerie meditates in a different fashion—by going to her car and listening to Grateful Dead tapes at heart-stopping volumes until the bad mood is blasted out of her head. My friend Leslie secretly consults her pocket-sized *I Ching* book. She says that the oracle's wisdom always helps her get through a difficult day.

All of these are simple solutions, of course, but I never can remember them when I'm in the middle of a stressful situation, so I carry Gladys's handy list with me—because sometimes things make more sense when they're written down.

BEND THE RULES

T his is a chapter about a three-letter-word that we often forget about when we're at work, and how to have more of it on the job. What I'm referring to, of course, is FUN. Who says that you can't get the work done *and* have a good time? Not Gladys A. Frumpworth IV, that's for sure! In this chapter, Gladys gives us permission to have fun—to bend the rules.

Did you ever blow giant, colorful bubbles in a drab office? Take treats to work and give an impromptu party? Leave confetti on somebody's desk? Give off a spontaneous howl? Post creative sayings on an office bulletin board? Draw pictures of Martians on somebody's whiteboard? Wear a gorilla mask to a job, even when it wasn't Halloween?

Gladys has done all of these things and more, with rave reviews. On one slow day she used the office intercom system to deliver innovative messages like "Frumpworth to Jones! Frumpworth to Jones! Come in, Jones! You have a call on line one thousand!" Another time she did a two-step on top of her desk, much to the delight of her weary co-workers, who gave her a standing ovation!

"By all means, dance on the desk," declares Gladys. "But do the right steps."

This means bend the rules, but keep in step with the situation. One company might be comfortable with a polka. Another, a tango. A third, a jig. Others may require a dance so slow that you don't feel like you're moving at all. Businesses and situations are as different as dance forms. Find the right form and you can bend the rules any time.

"How about a Watusi?" I asked Gladys, after returning home from one wild assignment.

To which she smiled and agreed that I had truly become a Temp from Hell.

It's important to reiterate that the Temp from Hell isn't a rebel. She doesn't break rules at random. She doesn't break rules just for the heck of it. On the contrary, she learns the rules, then bends them to the benefit of everyone involved. Of course, she follows the rules that say, "Be on time," and "Be courteous," and, certainly, "Do the work." On the other hand, she subscribes to her own rules:

❖ Have a sense of humor.
❖ Have fun.
❖ Be creative.
❖ Do whatever you can to make the day more positive for yourself and others.

And, yes, dance on the desk. But do the right steps.

Because temps are between jobs, between careers, between towns, or between ideas for the next phase of their lives, they are sometimes wary of doing things outside of the ordinary on jobs. They may feel vulnerable or uncertain as they travel in and out of assignments. They may feel that their supervisor has them on a leash. Guidelines can offer security. In the beginning of my temp career, I wouldn't have thought of howling in the middle of a busy office, much less dancing on a desk. I aimed to please. Drive a hundred miles on errands? Sure thing! Do work the second it hit the desk, no matter what else I was doing? You bet! Grow extra arms so that I could do multiple projects all at once? Well, just about.

Like most temps, I was in a period of transition. I was testing the temporary-employment waters. It was easier to be serious, to not rock the boat. All in earnest, of course. Until Gladys reminded me that it is possible to do a good job *and* have a good time.

Taking this cue, I did a little emotional jitterbugging on a credit hotline assignment at a medical supply company. My job was to take down "hot order" information on special yellow sheets of paper and shuffle them personally to credit account representatives.

When the reps saw that the orders were yellow, they knew that they were hot, and required to be processed in thirty minutes.

To make the work more fun for myself and others, I wrote the orders in red pen, drew flames around the pertinent information, and added short messages such as "Hot as heck," "Burning up!" and "Needs a potholder." For orders from Texas, I scrawled "Texas Hot" across the top. The reps usually responded with a laugh.

On my last day, when I made the rounds to say good-bye to people, one of the more serious people told me, "I want you to know that you really brightened my days. Those hot orders are interruptions, and your humor made it easier to deal with the pressure. It helped me look at my job in a new light."

It's amazing what a little innocent fun can do to break the ice.

I've since had numerous experiences where otherwise conservative people have told me how much they appreciated my approach, that it hadn't occurred to them to have fun at work. "Fun!" they muse. "What a revelation!"

If your internal office etiquette adviser warns that you can't be efficient when you're having a good time, tell him or her to chill out. Remind her or him that people actually work better when they feel good about themselves. Why trudge through the day when it's possible to dance, to bend the rules, to have fun? Do whatever feels right. Do whatever works. What better opportunity to offer this gift to all those serious and harried office workers around you?

Of course, there are businesses where you will never get out of a routine two-step, no matter how hard you try, because the tone is set from the top. If the top executive is a direct descendant of a rock, a stoneface who never smiles, it might be better to save your Watusi and rumba for another time. On the other hand, I recently had a conversation with one of those executives—someone I would have sworn was a relative of granite—during which I jokingly suggested that the center part of the office be turned into a dance floor to help relieve job-related tension. His dry response was, "It seems to me that you dance through just about everything you do." Then he broke into a smile and admitted that I had livened things up for him. So you never know what a little fun will bring. Which leads me to believe that in most cases it's at least okay to blow a few bubbles and sneak in a slow waltz.

SURVIVING JOB LULLS

S uddenly, you're a teenager all over again, waiting by the telephone for that certain call. Waiting for the date that hasn't happened all week. Picking up the receiver just in case the phone forgot to ring. Feeling anxious. Feeling ridiculous. You thought those crazy days were over. And who ever heard of dating a *temporary agency?*

Job lulls. If you're on a steady diet of temporary work, they're bound to occur at some point, sometimes when you least expect them. According to an informal survey of several temporary workers, there doesn't seem to be a particular pattern to these lulls. While some temps report a lack of work during holidays or summers, others find those times the most fruitful. Some temps work more in the summer and winter, some in the spring and fall. The abundance or lack of temporary work seems to depend mostly on:

❖ *Your type of work.* Retail and packaging jobs are plentiful during the holidays, while offices may gear down. Agricultural jobs and office assignments abound in the summer. Winters offer ski resort work. Universities require extra help in various capacities at the beginning of semesters.

❖ *Your temporary agency.* Different agencies tend to have different kinds of clients. One agency's clients may be busier in the spring and fall. Another agency may work mostly with businesses that are busy in summer.

❖ *Your geographical location.* There are more jobs in metropolitan areas, therefore more possibilities of keeping busy.

❖ *Your flexibility.* If you have a wide range of skills, are willing to travel to another town, and are open to a variety of assignments, you have a better chance of avoiding lulls.

❖ *Your persistence.* Sometimes you can't wait for work to come to you. You have to seek it out.

The fact is that, even when you do your best, job lulls *do* occur. The trick is not to let them get you down. Have you:

❖ *Called the agency more frequently?* Some temps report that calling an agency twice a day can help keep you at the top of the job list.
❖ *Made contacts on your own—new clients or previous ones?* Someone may have some work that you wouldn't have known about if you didn't call.
❖ *Signed up with a new agency?* This can be an energy-booster, as well as a new contact. Besides, the new agency may have work right at this moment, while your usual agency is in a lull.
❖ *Called companies where you've previously worked?* The fact that people know you may help to generate work.
❖ *Been willing to take a lower-paying assignment, just to tide you over?* Sometimes it only takes a few days of a lesser-paying assignment before something comes up requiring your skills.
❖ *Checked the want-ads in the newspaper? Checked community bulletin boards?* You never know where work might pop up.
❖ *Called to see if you are eligible for short-term unemployment benefits?* In some states, you may be eligible for unemployment compensation in as little as a week of no assignments. Contact your temporary agency or the state unemployment insurance office for specifics.

With applied vigor, one of these approaches should work within a few days. If a job doesn't immediately materialize, however, make sure that your answering machine is on, and:

❖ Do all the (cheap) things that you couldn't do if you were at work. Visit art galleries on free-admission days. Go to bargain matinees. Bake cookies, garden, or do 10,000-piece jigsaw puzzles. (Hint: if you can't think of anything to do, wait until your next job. You'll rack up a list the length of your street in no time!)

❖ Get some exercise. Go for walks or bike rides. Go roller-blading. Head for the nearest recreation center and do a few laps in the pool. Physical exercise is also good for emotional well-being.

❖ Do chores that you can never find time for when you're working. Organize closets, shampoo rugs, clean out the car, or give the dog a bath.

❖ Catch up with yourself. Get a haircut, begin a new exercise program, make a dental appointment, or take a relaxing bath.

❖ Learn something new. Go to the library and take out a book on something that you were always interested in but never got around to. Gladys A. Frumpworth IV learned massage therapy techniques during one job lull. Valerie took up hang-gliding.

❖ Do community work. Getting involved with the world outside of your house sometimes takes the edge off of job lulls. Pick up litter around the neighborhood. Visit someone in a nursing home. Volunteer in a soup kitchen for a day or two. Go grocery shopping for a community food-share program.

❖ Sell or donate items that you no longer need. Clean out your closets and make some money at the same time. Have a yard sale. Sell old books to a used bookstore, and take old clothes to the Salvation Army. You'll be grateful to yourself later.

Whatever you choose to do, it feels better to be productive during times off. Also, if you can afford a little luxury between assignments, alleviate the tension by doing something completely silly. Sometimes playing with wind-up toys or blowing soap bubbles can cheer up a job-lull day. Gladys is fond of playing loud music and dancing around the living room with her cat. Another temp I know falls back on a coloring book and crayons. Someone else feasts his eyes on his ever-growing collection of Mickey Mouses. "Just look at that Mickey!" he exclaims. "You know things can't be all bad with a happy guy like him in the world!"

Sometimes a break can be a blessing in disguise.

My friend Tina once spent a work-free month lying in bed, drinking herbal tea, and reading travel books. Although she was anxious in the beginning, after she figured out how long she could live on her bank balance, she decided to go with the flow.

"Sure, I was living on the edge," she admitted, "but it was one of the most therapeutic months I ever spent. I feel more rested than I've been in years."

Of course, job lulls can be periods of anxiety. They can also provide necessary breaks, or a warning to better prepare for the next lull. Either way, the telephone *will* eventually ring. And it will probably be the date that you've been waiting for.

SEXUAL HARASSMENT

O n my third day of one particular temp job, a chief executive officer of the company invited me to lunch.

"Some of us go every Friday," he said. "It would be fun if you could come along."

My first reaction was positive. I wasn't used to being asked to lunch by executives, and I thought, "How considerate of him to ask."

Then came the clincher.

"Clothing is optional for women," he added with a wink.

Having had no similar experience in fifty-odd assignments, I didn't have a clever comeback. Instead, I responded with a look of surprise, mixed with disgust. "No thanks," I muttered, and went out for a walk.

Once outside, I conjured up Gladys A. Frumpworth IV and asked her advice. She'd had an assignment at a law office that handled a sexual harassment case, so I figured she would recognize harassment when she saw it. Had I been harassed? I wanted to know. Or was this kind of behavior generally acceptable in the workplace these days? Was I being hypersensitive? She listened attentively, shook her head, and assured me that this wasn't to be confused with Romance on the Job. Then she told me what she knew.

According to the Code of Federal Regulations, Title 7 of the Civil Rights Act of 1964, Sexual Harassment is defined as follows:

Unwelcome sexual advances, requests for sexual favors, and other verbal or physical conduct of a sexual nature constitutes sexual harassment when: (1) submission to such conduct is made either explicitly or implicitly a term or condition of an individual's employment; (2) submission to or rejection of such conduct by an individual is used as the basis for employment decisions affecting such individuals; or (3) such conduct has the purpose or effect of unreasonably interfering with an individual's work performance or creates an intimidating, hostile, or offensive work environment.

After asking Gladys to repeat the third point, I nodded. Yes, I thought, I had definitely been sexually harassed. But what recourse did I have?

As a temporary employee, it would have been appropriate for me to contact my temporary agency, request a new assignment, and let them handle the incident, which is what I actually did. I also had the right to pursue the following course of action, as advised by the Equal Employment Opportunity Commission (EEOC):

1. Enlist the aid of a co-worker as a witness, and approach the harasser with your complaint. Be as specific as possible. Also, document the incident(s) in writing, in the event that you might need the details later.
2. If the harassment doesn't immediately cease, take the complaint to your supervisor. If the harasser is your supervisor, go to the supervisor's supervisor.
3. In the event that the situation is not handled by the supervisor's supervisor, file a complaint with the company's director of human resources.
4. If the situation is still not rectified, file a formal complaint with either the EEOC (listed under United States Government offices in the telephone book) or the Office of Civil Rights. These offices will advise you of your rights and conduct a full investigation.

The EEOC recommends that a complaint be registered for *any* incident of sexual harassment, because it is likely that the individual will approach others. The commission received a record of more than ten thousand harassment claims in 1992 alone, although surveys reveal that less than 5 percent of those being harassed actually file.

In my case, I subsequently discovered that the chief executive officer's attitude was prevalent in that company. Prominent on many of the men's office doors was a supposedly humorous poster that was derogatory to women. There were "anatomically correct" birthday cakes, inappropriate photographs on the walls, and sexually explicit jokes. Feeling uncomfortable with this, I spoke with a few female employees, who admitted similar discomfort. No one wanted to complain for fear of jeopardizing their jobs. As a temp, I could leave any time, without ill effects. As it turned out, "any time" was the day following the harassment.

Fortunately, more businesses are now taking measures to train their employees in harassment prevention and to emphasize more sensitive work environments. This includes awareness of the need to be more discerning in language and actions in the workplace. Federal and state laws protect *all* employees, and companies are bound to abide by them. Some cities and counties have their own laws regarding this serious offense. In addition, the National Organization for Women (NOW) and numerous local groups are also working to bring the issue to the forefront.

Harassment can happen to anyone. I recently spoke with a temp who had to end an assignment in a medical office when one of the doctors began to unbutton the back of her blouse.

"When I asked what he was doing, he replied that I looked too serious that day and he wanted to 'wake me up,' " she told me. "I was really shocked. I'm a *grandmother*, for goodness' sake! I informed him that I must be too serious to work there at all, and I left right away."

So, harassment can even happen to grandmothers. It can also happen to men. As Gladys points out, men are not the only offenders. During her tenure at the law office, Gladys heard of a woman who pulled down her pants in the middle of a busy department in order to show off a monkey tattoo on her right knee. The next day an offended male co-worker filed a complaint.

HEALTH TIPS

Your eyeballs feel stir-fried, and your hands are an advertisement for Arthritic Gumby. Your shoulders are bent into a perpetual vulture posture. Your throat is sore, your elbows are turning blue, and your back is one big ache. Not only this, but your brain feels ready to burst right out of your head. You suspect that you have *it*.

You probably do.

Gladys A. Frumpworth IV often jokes about what she calls Brain Fungus Disease, the mush that your brain becomes when you work with computers all day, although health risks related to these wonder machines are actually nothing to laugh about. Sitting in front of a computer screen seems so easy that a person can do it for hours without taking a break. Therein lies the problem. There are things to watch out for, she cautions. Being very health-conscious, Temps from Hell tries to disseminate tips whenever possible. Here are some letters that Gladys has received:

Dear Gladys,

When I'm at my computer, I sometimes hear my neck humming the funeral march. It begins very softly, then gets louder throughout the day. Finally, I can't ignore it, and I get up for a cup of coffee. At this point, there seems to be an audible sigh, and the humming stops. When I return to my computer, it resumes. I've tried earplugs, but they don't block out the sound. Do you think I'm crazy?

Hearing Voices

Dear Voices,

Your problem sounds like a pain in the neck! Tell me, is your neck also *sore*? Do your shoulders and back ache? Sometimes a body bent over a computer for many hours will do *anything* to get attention—like humming the funeral march, for instance! Try to be aware of your neck when it's under stress. Make it happy by giving it an adjustable chair with back support and arm rests. Adjust the chair until it is the correct height for the computer table or desk. Stand up frequently and stretch. Do neck exercises by rolling your head in a circular motion. It will soon be singing a different tune, possibly something like "You Are My Sunshine."

Dear Temps from Hell,

Can I get sunburned from my computer screen? If so, what number of sunscreen should I use? Would you advise sunglasses?

Goggle-eyed

Dear Goggle-eyed,

Actually, the Temps from Hell has been known to wear sunglasses from time to time while she was working on computer because the glare from computer screens can be hard on the eyes. Of course, she sometimes wears a sequined beret or deely-boppers on the job, too, when she's feeling silly.

Project your eyes as much as possible by blinking frequently. Take five or ten minutes away from your screen each hour. Put adjustable blinds on your windows to regulate glare from outside. If eyestrain is a problem, rest your eyes at intervals by closing them, and apply a cold cloth on the eyelids. Find an activity that doesn't require the use of your eyes for a while. Sleep, or play Blind Man's Bluff.

P.S. Try a sunscreen with SPF #15. But use it outside, not at your computer.

Dear Gladys A. Frumpworth IV.

I've admired you for a long time, and I'm wondering if you have a twin. My own alter ego got injured on the job, and I feel kind of lost. Are temps covered by Workers' Compensation?

Deserted

Dear Deserted,

Oh, dear! I'm sorry about your alter ego; alas, I have no twin. There is only one Gladys A. Frumpworth IV. If your alter ego was indeed injured in a work situation, he or she should be covered by Workers' Compensation. Speak to the human resources department of your workplace, or contact your temporary agency. If the injury is of an emotional nature, consult the "Stress!" or "When to Bail Out" chapter in this book.

Dear Gladys,

I am pregnant, and my unborn child keeps complaining that my visual display terminal is too bright. Do you think this means that he will be a Temp from Hell?

Mom

Dear Mom,

I hope so! The more Temps from Hell, the better. But, as far as the terminal goes, your child may be right. Many physicians warn against prolonged computer exposure for pregnant women. Computer screens do generate a small amount of radiation. Tell your young hellion that you will consult your doctor about this pronto.

Dear Gladys,

My wrists have been sore lately, and typing seems to make them worse. When I wake up in the morning, I often experience a tingling sensation in my fingers and my arms. I share my computer at work with a woman who has similar symptoms. She suspects that she has arthritis. Is arthritis contagious? Is it possible that I caught her arthritis from the keyboard?

Worried

Dear Worried,

So far, arthritis isn't contagious. Do you also have purple spots on your ankles and green stripes on your head? If not, this is no joking matter, as you and your co-worker may have carpal tunnel syndrome, a serious wrist-and-hand disorder that is caused by repetitive motion (as in typing or factory production work). Tendons in the wrist become inflamed, and the tunnel of eight bones bound by ligaments narrows. This puts pressure on the nerves, leading to pain, numbness, and a tingling or burning sensation in the fingers and thumbs.

To protect yourself from carpal tunnel, use a keyboard at elbow height and a contoured wrist support. Keep your typing speed down, and regularly stretch your hands and wrists.

If you develop symptoms, stop all repetitive motion, and massage your wrists or go to a massage therapist. To reduce swelling, apply ice or soak your hands in cold water. Aspirin relieves inflammation. Vitamin B_6 has also been said to alleviate symptoms. Experiment with wrist braces. Of course, if the problem persists, see a doctor. Also experiment with changing occupations. Become an astronaut or a guidance counselor.

Dear Temps from Hell,

I have a new temp job in a factory where sticky multicolored bubbles regularly fill the building. They are as large as basketballs and smell like different flavors of bubble gum. They are so thick that the workers can't even see each other. Many of us have developed giggly laughs, runny eyes, and the urge to sing children's songs at the top of our lungs. Is this an occupational hazard that we should be concerned about?

Bub at the Bubble Gum Factory

Dear Bub,

I wish I could have a temp job at your bubble gum factory. It sounds like fun. However, if any assignment requires exposure to substances that you aren't familiar with, it's a good idea to find out what they are. Strong chemicals, cigarette smoke, or radiation-producing machines are indeed health hazards. Make sure that your work area is properly ventilated and that safety rules are posted. Also, wear the necessary clothing, shoes, and headgear—in your case, stick-proof!

Gladys A. Frumpworth IV can't say enough about how important it is for temps to protect themselves from health hazards on the job, computer-related or otherwise. She suggests that you consult your physician or temporary agency if you have questions. No job is worth seriously jeopardizing your health.

KNOW WHEN TO COVER YOURSELF

I was introduced to the concept of covering myself by a seasoned executive secretary who had her boss look over everything before it went out. Letters. Reports. Office supply orders. She gave him the last word on every minute detail. She also kept specific reports of petty cash and insisted that all requests be okayed by the chief financial officer.

As a novice temp, I thought she was oversolicitous or suffering from lack of self-confidence, which seemed surprising in a person who'd had about a hundred years of office experience. In every other way this woman was a real go-getter, the kind of person that Gladys A. Frumpworth IV truly admired. Why, I wondered, was she so meek on this issue? So, after watching her boss check her work for the millionth time, I pressed for an explanation.

"Why not just get it out yourself?" I wanted to know.

To which she replied in a knowing voice, "Cover yourself."

"Cover yourself?"

"Absolutely," she said. "I don't want it to be *my* fault if a large order comes in that no one wants. If the boss signs for it, then it's *his* problem if something isn't the way he wants it. The same for letters. If he reads them over, he is more apt to catch a phrase that he didn't really mean to say. And I'm covered."

At the time I thought this "cover yourself" was ridiculous. It seemed like a lack of initiative on the secretary's part, or unwillingness to take responsibility for her own actions. Or worse, paranoia. I didn't get it. That evening I decided to ask Gladys if she had ever heard of such a thing.

I found her in the kitchen, baking a batch of oatmeal chocolate-chip cookies to take to a temporary job the next day. She was wearing a Temps from Hell apron, which sported a picture of a grinning devil toasting marshmallows on a pitchfork over a bonfire. Gladys popped a warm cookie into my mouth and nodded. Then she served up the following ways for temps to cover themselves on the job:

❖ Don't be responsible for large amounts of cash or personal checks.
❖ Don't sign for expensive items.
❖ Don't sign someone else's name to a document.
❖ Don't drive someone else's car.
❖ Don't allow yourself to be the only person on the premises if you sense that the clients are distrustful for any reason.
❖ Don't make the decision to do something illegal, such as making photocopies of copyrighted materials.
❖ Don't repeat information. If someone tells you something about the company or an employee, keep it to yourself.
❖ Don't congregate in the open with other temporary employees during work hours.

After listening to Gladys's list, I had to agree that the items made obvious sense, although I was puzzled by the last one. "What difference does it make if temps socialize?" I asked. "Isn't it good that they can give each other moral support?"

A buzzer went off, and Gladys took a tray from the oven with her red Temps from Hell mitts.

"We already know that employers are a little wary of a temporary worker," she explained. "From their viewpoint, a temp talking to a permanent employee is discussing work. But a temp talking to another temp is interpreted as work not getting done, which means that the company's money is being wasted. Therefore, if temps avoid congregating in the open, they won't arouse distrust."

"I never thought of that," I said.

Gladys nodded. "Most employers don't know what it's like to be a temp because they've never been one. Moral support among temporary workers probably doesn't occur to them. So it's best to cover yourself."

Temporary agencies seem to agree. In fact, they even issue a disclaimer to clients, stating that temporary workers shall not be responsible for unattended premises, cash, and other valuables or negotiables. Accounting temps are not allowed to sign their names to financial statements or tax returns. The disclaimer also maintains that temporary employees shall not operate machinery or motor vehicles without prior written permission of the agency.

This doesn't imply that temps aren't responsible employees. It only indicates that temporary positions don't involve such responsibilities. Generally, temps don't have to think about these issues because they rarely present themselves. For me personally, the subject has come up on very few occasions. Those occasions were enough to convince me that the executive secretary who first introduced this "cover yourself" advice had the right idea. I heard the following story from another temp, who learned the wisdom of "cover yourself" from an awkward situation.

Bill had been on an accounting assignment for two months when, without warning, he was accused of stealing a roll of stamps, which had mysteriously disappeared from the office manager's desk. Having had no such previous experience, he wondered what he had done to provoke the accusation. As it turned out, the office manager had miscalculated the last time she bought a roll. This was only the beginning.

The situation rapidly escalated as Bill was subsequently suspected of taking a box of stick pens worth ninety-nine cents (discovered in the president's office) . . . stealing coffee from the refrigerator (the manager forgot that there had been several visiting clients that week) . . . charging airline tickets on the company account for personal use (there was no proof) . . . and taking an important check out of the mailbox, although the office manager was the only one who had a key. All this within a time span of a few weeks. It was definitely a "cover yourself" situation.

After experiencing a mixture of anger and disbelief, Bill decided that there was a paranoia problem with either the office manager or the company itself. He then accepted the hopelessness of the circumstances and ended the assignment.

As Bill discovered, how you cover yourself on an assignment

depends on the nature of the company. If the clients seem particularly nervous about trusting temporary employees or any employees, you'll need to be more on guard, or leave the job altogether. The best judge of this is your intuition. When I told Gladys about Bill's experience, she was filling a plastic storage box with the oatmeal chocolate-chip cookies. She thought that it made sense to exercise caution, but she didn't think that temps should be paranoid. Then she handed me the box of warm cookies.

"Help yourself," she grinned. "But please put the cover back on when you're finished."

WHEN TO BAIL OUT

I n the dream, I was peacefully sleeping in my own bed, when I heard a loud explosion outside. I ran to the bedroom window and saw that the sky was filled with smoke. Weird green animals with glowing red eyes were running around the front yard, frothing at the mouth and biting each other. Suddenly, a group of environmental activists appeared. Carrying signs and torches, they marched down the street and up my driveway. They pounded on the front door and shouted for me to come out. They were about to set fire to the house when I awoke.

As I sat up in bed and wiped the sweat off my forehead, I saw that it was morning. The sun was shining, and the sky was fairybook blue. Birds sang. Squirrels chattered. My head was still filled with angry skies and grotesque green creatures, however, and I realized that this was the fifth such nightmare of the week. I looked at the clock. It was time to go to my current temporary job—at a nuclear power plant—and tell them that I was bailing out.

It's not always obvious when it's time to end an assignment. Particularly if the business environment is pleasant, the work is satisfying, the people are nice—and you seriously need the money. But when a job gets to you on a personal or ethical level, you can usually count on some sign to tattle that you've had enough.

Everyone has a different sign. One temp friend of mine keeps track of her toleration level by a sporadic outbreak of hives. When the first spots appear, she figures she's edging toward the brink. By the time she can no longer count them, she's out the door. Another friend, against his will, yells at his beloved golden retriever. My friend Valerie craves shark, which, *she swears*, only occurs when she's at the end of her temporary job rope. This makes sense, she reasons, on the basis of cause and effect. She explains: "I don't usually eat shark because I like to swim in the ocean. If *I* eat shark, then maybe a shark will come along and think it's okay to eat *me*. Therefore, when I crave shark, I know it means that I'm in a situation where I'm asking to be eaten alive."

I can't remember when I last craved shark, but my dreams seem to be fairly reliable signals. The dream cited at the beginning of this chapter was related to a technical drawing project that was geared toward the reopening of a nuclear power plant in the Denver area. My job was to draw charts of dump sites and outline data containing nuclear jargon—a fairly involved and creative assignment, despite the subject matter.

On the day of the dream, I was asked to design a cover page for the project report: a drawing of the nuclear plant nestled against a clip-art picture of animals frolicking in a mountain forest. I recall a lot of physical tension as I worked (clenching my jaw, holding my breath). I was painfully aware of my membership in certain environmental organizations. I ignored these signs, especially after mentioning them to my project partners (also temps), who teased me for being hypersensitive and "politically correct." Wasn't the money the most important thing? After all, it was "good money" *and* near Christmas, a time when other assignments might be scarce.

Admitting that they made some good arguments, I continued to work in silence. My internal tensions worsened. Also, I missed having Gladys for moral support and companionship. Yes, the truth is that even faithful Gladys deserted me during this stressful period, disapproving as she was of my decision. So my dreams took over. And took over some more, until I could no longer ignore them. After I gave notice, the nightmares promptly stopped.

Bail out if:

❖ You are threatened verbally, physically, or sexually.
❖ You become sick more than usual.
❖ You suddenly suffer from chronic stress symptoms, such as constant headaches, hives, or fatigue that disappears as soon as you leave the job site.
❖ You become aware of physical tension, such as holding your breath, making fists, clenching your jaws, or grinding your teeth.
❖ Your personality changes uncharacteristically to compensate for the situation—for example, you become depressed, angry, or emotionally "shut down."
❖ You feel increasingly uneasy in the surroundings. You have a bad feeling that you can't quite put your finger on.
❖ You find yourself frequently crying.
❖ You develop physical symptoms related to the work, such as carpal tunnel syndrome, high pressure in your eyes, allergic reactions to chemicals, smoke, etc. (Gladys once had to leave a work site because she was allergic to the woman sitting next to her, who wore "killer perfume.")
❖ You have nightmares of any duration.

If a company's motivation feels wrong, or the people are unusually difficult, or the work itself seems dangerous, your intuition will somehow let you know that it's time to bail out. This happened to Gayle when she worked an assignment at a company that was in the middle of massive layoffs. Every day more and more people were let go, while she, as a temp, was encouraged to remain. Tensions mounted all around, as Gayle pondered finding another assignment. On the day that co-workers broke out shouting and a heavy book was thrown at the wall, missing her by inches, Gayle decided that she had had enough. She told me later: "When the book hit the wall, I had an instantaneous vision of a fly being killed by a fly swatter. I guess it was the sound that did it—*splat!* At the time it seemed like a silly thought, but I guess my subconscious was trying to let me know that that fly could easily be me."

When Gayle gave notice, her supervisor tried to talk her out of her decision, assuring her that tensions would pass and layoffs would end. The work environment would once again be peaceful, he said. In fact, did she want a job? She was a reliable worker and there would soon be openings to fill. But Gayle stayed with her gut feeling. She kept seeing herself as the fly on the wall—and, as it turned out, a fly who flew away before the fly swatter had its chance.

Gladys, having now thankfully returned, urges temps to listen to themselves when they feel the need to bail out. Don't let anyone talk you out of your decision. Not your friends, family, or temporary agency. Who wants to be at the mercy of a fly swatter?

If you must stay in an unhealthy situation for financial reasons, find ways to alleviate the stress until you can get out. Talk to a friend. Walk. Sing. Anything. Look seriously for another assignment and, when one materializes, take it pronto. No assignment is worth risking your mental or physical health. Or—heaven forbid—worth losing the loyalty of a good alter ego like Gladys A. Frumpworth IV. Don't wait for an explosion, nuclear or otherwise. Bail out!

GETTING FIRED

Before my friend Tina called to say that she had been fired from her current assignment, I was stuffing pasta shells for a Temps from Hell meeting and talking to Gladys A. Frumpworth IV about the variety of temporary jobs that a temp has. We imagined each job as a separate stage, with changing characters and the temp playing a pivotal role. We considered how differently each person sees you in your role. Some think you're charming. Some view you as a teacher. Some see you as a valuable part of the work team. A few of those characters fall madly in love with you, while others barely take notice. And, unfortunately, some don't like you at all.

When I picked up the receiver on the third ring, the voice on the other end was already running a marathon.

"I got fired!" Tina cried. "After only four days! Do you believe it? It was supposed to go for two months. And they were so *nice* to me, too! But today when I went to pick up my check, they said that they needed someone who could work faster. I thought everything was going along fine. What should I do?"

"Come right over," I told her as I stuffed spinach into a large shell. "We're just about to have a Temps from Hell meeting. It will make you feel better to talk about it."

As I drizzled marinara sauce over the shells and put them in the oven, Gladys got out extra dishes and a fresh box of Kleenex. Shortly thereafter, the doorbell rang, and the meeting began.

Getting fired. . . . Being laid off. . . . Terminated. . . . Job-declared-excess. Nobody likes it, whatever it's called. Nevertheless, it happens all the time. Tina had been temping at an urban telemarketing firm where the pace is fast and the competition furious. The employees were required to make a minimum of ten calls an hour, which was high even for Tina, a seasoned telemarketer. They were also required to put a lot of sales pressure on the people they called. By nature, Tina is a quiet, laid-back person who likes to *talk* to the people she calls. I could see why she didn't fit in.

What my friend was upset about was not so much that the job had ended, but that the ending had been out of her control and that she had been personally rejected. Never mind that she couldn't be more opposite in values from the people at the firm. Never mind that she had felt suffocated there. No matter that she had already complained about how much she disliked the job. It's funny how all that logic disappears when you're faced with something like the stigma of getting fired.

People are often surprised when they hear about temps being disappointed when a job is terminated. Why bother? they wonder. Isn't the whole point of temporary work to not be attached to the situation? To walk away relatively unscathed? Won't the temp just go on to a new assignment and quickly forget the old situation? While all of these points are accurate, the truth remains that being fired *hurts*, whether you're a temporary or a permanent employee. For instance, temps still go through the emotional stages that people normally experience when they are "liberated" from a situation:

1. Anger. "How *dare* they fire me!"
2. Hurt. "Didn't they like me?"
3. Denial. "This didn't really happen, did it?"
4. Sadness. "It happened all right, and it's too bad."
5. Letting go of any attachment to the job. "It's over, so I may as well figure out the next step."
6. Moving on to a new job. "I really like it here. This is the job I should have had in the first place."

The difference is that a temp may require less time to get over being fired, since there was probably less time invested in the work and fewer emotions invested in the people. The temp moves more quickly through the phases before taking on a new job. But no matter the timing, having a job ended for us is never easy because our tendency is to try to fit successfully into an employment situation, to make things work.

"We want to end assignments when *we* choose, not when *they* choose," we stated in the Temps from Hell meeting, between bites of pasta.

"Of course," agreed Gladys, "but what we forget at the time is that getting fired is often an opportunity for growth. That getting fired can be a chance to *get fired up* toward something new."

Which is exactly what Tina did. After spending a few days working through the first several phases, including screaming, crying, running several miles, and getting plenty of extra sleep, she called her temporary agency to request a new assignment. Two weeks later, secure in a position that she liked, she was able to admit that everything had worked out for the best. Two *years* later, she had gone through twenty or thirty more temp jobs, and several translation projects. Her next plan was to move to Japan to teach English.

At another Temps from Hell meeting, Tina recalled the incident of being fired from the telemarketing firm. By then, it seemed like a stepping stone to her real goals.

"It's amazing to think how upset I was," she said. "I didn't even like the job! If I had stayed with it, I would have missed out on some important translation work, not to mention a teaching job."

"All of the people can't like you all of the time," we said in unison, in our imitation Gladys voices. "And we can't always be the piece that completes the company's jigsaw puzzle. Sometimes we're the wrong shape altogether."

"Bravo!" Gladys applauded in response. Of course, Gladys would understand. She was once fired from a position, with two weeks' notice. Did she get angry? Yes. Did she feel hurt? Sure. Was there sadness and denial? You bet. By her last day on the job, Gladys had worked well past letting go. On that day she dressed up, took a bottle of champagne to work, and gave herself a going-away party. Then she thanked everyone for a truly interesting experience, and moved on to her true destiny—as the Temp from Hell.

THE LAST DAY

L ast days. And more last days. When you work temporary, there are always more. As Gladys the Wise says, "Give me a last day, and I'll soon give you another first day." And so the cycle continues.

Each final day on a job is different. I've had last days where people have taken me out to appreciation lunches, and last days that have passed without incident. A lot of this depends on the duration of the assignment. Obviously, there is going to be more sentiment involved in the last day of a three-month job than in the last day of a three-day job, simply because there is more opportunity to establish relationships. One woman gave me a hug when I wrapped up a two-month assignment, and, as I assured her that her new assistant would be great, she burst into tears and sniffled, "But it won't be *you!*" At the end of another long-term job, my supervisor read aloud a list of the reasons why he had enjoyed working with me. At the same time, I've had many assignments, mostly short-term, where my co-workers weren't even around to say goodbye.

I've left some jobs with teary farewells and others with secret pleasure mixed with relief. I've made good friends and valuable contacts. And, yes, a foe or two. It all varies according to the company, its employees, and the individual temp—the unique recipe of each situation.

But last days are more than goodbyes. There is still plenty of work to do.

❖ Write a detailed note to your supervisor, or the person you are replacing, concerning the status of all projects. Include next steps and/or questions that you may have. If your work is computerized, make a list of the documents by file name.

❖ Inform people that you're leaving. This is a courtesy to let them know what to expect. A simple memo on a bulletin board a few days prior to your departure, or a message via electronic mail, is fine. Or, if there are few people to notify, speaking to them directly is more personal.

❖ Find out if there are loose ends that you need to tie up before you go. Ask around. Someone may feel more comfortable if you finish up the details of a particular project rather than asking a new person to jump into unfamiliar territory.

❖ If requested, agree to train your "successor." Keep the training basic. The company can provide specifics later. Be prepared to give the person a building tour, introduce him or her to the staff, answer any questions, and explain duties required of the position.

❖ If you use a computer, make sure that everything is in order. The files should be easy to find and backed up on floppy disks or tapes. Any personal letters or documents should be removed. Gladys has found passionate love letters and other intimate correspondence left on business computers by temps. While *she* actually enjoys reading them, she knows that she would feel quite embarrassed for someone else to read such a personal item of her own.

❖ Leave only positive traces of yourself.
  —Make sure that the work space and files are clean and in order. (I usually spend a few minutes wiping off the desk and equipment.)
  —Take everything that is yours, even the smallest things. On one of Gladys's last days, she ate a sesame seed roll at her desk, then spent several minutes digging out the seeds that fell between the cracks!
  —If you feel so inclined, leave a gift for the person who is returning. It doesn't have to be large. Think about how much someone might enjoy being greeted by a "Welcome back" sign, an origami crane, a chocolate-chip cookie, or a single flower in a vase.

Now come the goodbyes.

If you become easily attached to people or situations, this may be the hardest part of a temporary assignment. Gladys warns that it is simpler to keep goodbyes low-key, genuinely wishing people good luck and remembering that you will be moving on. There is always the option of keeping in touch. Leaving a job doesn't have to mean permanent separation from new friends. It's possible to keep up telephone calls and luncheon dates well beyond the last day of an assignment. Not to mention enduring friendships that may be enjoyed several years later.

A word about last days when you have had to terminate a job, or when the assignment has not been pleasant: try to leave as quietly as possible. It is always important to leave on a positive note, if you can, without burning bridges. To shake hands and wish even difficult people the best. Gladys had one assignment where she had a serious personality conflict with her supervisor. On her last day, this man smiled warmly and announced that he was sorry she was leaving. Although she felt tempted to dispute his obvious insincerity, she thanked him through gritted teeth, shook his hand, and hoped that he would be more compatible with the next temp.

As Gladys says, "After the goodbyes, even difficult ones, there will be many more hellos. You can count on most of those goodbyes and hellos to be pleasant." Well said, Gladys. She nods in response—and is off to another hot assignment.

GOING PERMANENT

W e got dressed up and had our last Temps from Hell meeting at the Ritz, in honor of Valerie, who was "going permanent." Between Valerie, who didn't seem very happy, and Gladys A. Frumpworth IV, who kept trying to get up and help the waitress, I had my hands full.

"Aren't you excited about your new job?" I asked Valerie. "Paid benefits? Real money? A chance to establish rapport with one group of people?"

"Yes," Valerie said, "but it feels weird not being a temp anymore. I've been a temp for years. I'm *used* to being a temp. And I won't be able to come to these meetings!"

After Gladys and I assured her that she had a standing invitation to all Temps from Hell meetings, our meal arrived—fancy sandwiches, Caesar salads, and a bottle of Chardonnay. We toasted Valerie, Gladys tried to talk the waitress into joining us for a short break, and we began to discuss this business of "going permanent."

Many temporary workers such as Valerie use short-term assignments as stepping stones to permanent employment. Temping can be a good way to assess a company, to get an idea of the people who work there and decide if it's really where you want to be before making a long-term commitment. It's a wonderful opportunity for getting your foot in the door without going through the process of interviewing in an unfamiliar situation. In Valerie's case, she temped in the accounting department at a large corporation, where her position was designed to go permanent. As with many companies, her supervisor considered it an advantage to know beforehand the person that he hired.

While many temps assert that companies don't hire them because (a) businesses aren't interested in finding out the temp's skills or (b) "temps have a bad image," this isn't always true. Sometimes a supervisor isn't aware of a temp's qualifications, or doesn't realize that a temp wants to be hired. Temps can change this by taking responsibility through the following steps.

❖ *Let your agency know that you are looking for a full-time position.* They can send you on assignments that are designed to go permanent.

❖ *Be yourself.* Let the company get to know you as an individual. Don't allow anyone to slot you as "the temp" or even as "the Temp from Hell," without knowing your true nature. Pointedly but unobtrusively talk about yourself, your skills and background.

❖ *Do an excellent job.* It is the best PR that any temp can have.

❖ *Have a positive attitude.* This may be even more important than doing an excellent job. People hire people that they have rapport with. Remember Gladys, the cheerful hellion? She has been offered a full-time position at a majority of the companies she's temped for, and she isn't even looking for permanent employment!

❖ *Give a copy of your résumé to your supervisor.* Make sure that he or she is aware of what you have to offer to the position.

❖ *Express interest.* Learn everything you can about your job. Ask questions. Find out what advancement potential the job has, and determine which of your skills might fit in with such advancement.

❖ *Talk to the human resources department in the company.* You can initiate procedures by filling out an application, submitting your résumé, and getting to know the people who are liaisons in the hiring process. Keep your eye on job openings posted on company bulletin boards.

❖ *Network with supervisors and permanent employees.* Talk to people in your department and the company in general. Let them know that you're looking for a full-time position. There may be positions opening up that even human resources isn't aware of.

❖ *Network with other temps.* Generally temps know a lot about what's going on in the job market. Another temp may have information about openings in your current company, or in another company. Gladys was once approached with an offer by her immediate supervisor on an assignment. Although she wasn't interested, she gave him the name of a temp on another floor who was. By the time Gladys left, that temp was happily installed.

In the first item on the list, there is sometimes a slight catch to looking for full-time work through an agency. Because the agency usually charges a fee to employers, but not to the temp, some companies (usually small ones) feel that they can't afford to hire temporary workers. On the other hand, some large corporations hire *only* through temporary agencies. The advantage for them is that the agency screens prospective employees and sends them as temporaries. The corporation can then assess temps on the job before making a commitment.

Another common practice is that companies require "temp to perm" employees to work for a probation period of three to six months before they are eligible for "permanence." This is to evaluate the motivation of the potential employee, to see if his or her attitude and performance will endure. The corporation that hired Valerie required *all* employees (unless they were supervisors) to report as "leased workers" before a hiring decision would be made. The same corporation also had a thousand-hour limitation on temps; after the thousandth hour, they were either hired on or required to leave. Valerie likes to joke that she was hired after the 999th hour.

"A lot of temps go permanent from temporary," Gladys was telling Valerie as we were making decisions about dessert at the Ritz. "I know temps who seesaw between permanent jobs and temping, and temps who find a permanent situation and never do temporary work again."

This was true, Valerie and I agreed.

"It doesn't mean that either situation is preferable," Gladys continued. "It just happens to be what you're doing at the time." She chose an appropriately Temps from Hell dish—raspberry flambé—and poured more Chardonnay all around.

Valerie and I agreed again as we made our own choices, chocolate-swirl cheesecake and peach mousse. But Gladys didn't seem to be listening. Instead, she was offering a toast to the readers of this book.

"Goodbye and good luck," she said, lifting her glass.

ABOUT THE AUTHOR

My career began at birth, meaning that *I* am my career, that I try to give myself fully to everything I do. So far this has included ten years in publishing (writing and production/design for newspapers, magazines, and books), teaching preschool, conducting intake interviews in a county jail, and doing all kinds of temporary work in over one hundred businesses. Along the way, I acquired a B.A. in Writing Arts and Art from the State University of New York at Oswego, studied British literature at the University of London, did graduate studies in creative writing at the University of Colorado, and attended a multitude of writing conferences.

Most of my nonwork time is spent walking, doing Zen meditation practice, reading Japanese literature, watching spiders spin webs, and inviting the life stories of people, wherever I meet them.

Is this all? Mostly, and not nearly. Who knows what comes next? The possibilities are endless.